New Directions for Small-Group Ministry

by
Paul Borthwick
Carl F. George
Paul A. Kaak
Carol H. Lukens
Gary C. Newton
Steve R. Sheeley

Vital
MINISTRY™
Loveland, Colorado

New Directions for Small-Group Ministry

Visit our Web site: **www.grouppublishing.com**

Credits
Editor: Dennis McLaughlin
Chief Creative Officer: Joani Schultz
Copy Editor: Shirley Michaels
Art Director: Kari K. Monson
Cover Art Director: Jeff A. Storm
Cover Designer: Alan Furst, Inc. Art and Design
Computer Graphic Artist: Pat Miller
Production Manager: Peggy Naylor

Library of Congress Cataloging-in-Publication Data
New directions for small-group ministry / by Paul Borthwick ... [et al.]
      p.   cm.
   ISBN 0-7644-2137-9 (alk. paper)
   1. Church group work. 2. Small groups--Religious aspects-
-Christianity. I. Borthwick, Paul, 1954-   .
BV652.2N47 1999
253'.7--dc21   99-25742
                                       CIP

10 9 8 7 6 5 4 3 2 1   08 07 06 05 04 03 02 01 00 99

Contents

97705

INTRODUCTION

Introduction

New Directions

One of the problems with postmodernism is deciding which voices to listen to and which to trust. There are many people speaking, but how many are both relevant to today's people and true to God's Word? As a result, many church leaders are confused and unsure about which direction small-group ministries should take. When it comes down to it, the true test of knowing who to listen to is to answer the question, *Who's been successful in keeping small groups relevant and life changing in today's world?*

That's precisely why *New Directions for Small-Group Ministry* was developed and written by six small-group experts, or what postmodernism would term, *artists*. The six writers represent a handful of risk takers who successfully answered the postmodern challenge to be relevant. These writers represent a combined, trustworthy voice that small-group leaders and church leaders need to hear.

In Chapter 1, **Carol Lukens** tells an encouraging story about a successful small-group ministry that has stood the test of time by being flexible and by responding to where God is working in the life of the congregation. The real beauty of Carol's chapter is that she reminds us that God is still in charge. Lukens compellingly presents what she terms "a mosaic approach" to small-group ministry that calls for a diversity of groups to exist within the same congregation. According to Lukens, many small-group programs have been unsuccessful simply because their leaders try to funnel all groups into a single approach.

In Chapter 2, **Paul Borthwick**, a visionary for small groups involved in servant ministry, presents a strong case for the necessity of

4

groups to be involved in service. He suggests that for a small group to be vital, it must have a purpose larger than itself. According to Borthwick, small-group leaders need to challenge participants to contribute something beyond simple attendance at a weekly meeting. He believes that engaging participants in servant ministry is the key to life-changing growth in the small-group setting.

Chapter 3 is presented by **Dr. Gary Newton**, who tells of his rich experiences with small groups made up of participants from different age groups, from young children to senior adults. He admits that intergenerational experiences may at first seem awkward, but with a little time and work, they can become some of the most powerful and life-changing experiences in the life of any congregation.

In Chapter 4, **Paul Kaak** suggests that the majority of Generation X have turned away from traditional small-group programs because they believe them to be inauthentic, and he gets right to the heart of identifying how a small-group ministry can be relevant in the postmodern culture. Why dedicate an entire chapter to one generation? Because, as Kaak points out, Generation X will provide the next group of leaders charged with carrying the church into the future.

Chapter 5, written by small-group expert **Steve Sheeley**, is, in a sense, a bonus chapter. Sheeley challenges church leaders to move beyond a successful small-group program by asking why the life-changing experiences of small groups can't be incorporated into the whole church. Sheeley doesn't just talk theology. He presents a practical *needs-assessment* tool that can provide the foundation for a plan to integrate small-group dynamics throughout the whole church.

Finally, Chapter 6 was written by the father of metagroup ministry, **Carl George**. Carl identifies a diamond-mine opportunity for small groups that has long been overlooked, Sunday schools. He resists the critics who claim that Sunday schools can't deliver the intimacy of home Bible studies or prayer groups. As an appropriate conclusion to the book, Carl provides a sure-fire method of developing new small-group leadership.

A Final Note

In the past, success with a small-group program was based on a fixed model or a precise recipe. In a postmodern context, however, the formula for success is anything but fixed or precise. So what you'll notice as you digest the words of these six small-group *artists* is that none of them recommend a particular model or precise recipe for small-group success. Most significantly, however, you'll notice that these authors recognize that what God needs from small-group ministries today is different than what God needed from them yesterday.

Each author has been willing to take a risk by responding to the postmodern challenge. Each has crossed the abyss and made small groups relevant to the life of the modern church. Now, they invite you to do the same!

CHAPTER 1

Small Groups: A Mosaic From the Master's Hand

CAROL H. LUKENS

Carol Lukens serves as director of small groups at Asbury United Methodist Church in Tulsa, Oklahoma.

A Mosaic Approach to Small Groups

I sat on my porch on a crisp, clear autumn day and watched a brilliant red maple leaf float to the ground and join others that had already fallen. Some of the leaves were orange, others stood out as bright yellow, and some russet. I walked out to take a closer look at the leaf that had just fallen. But as I reached for it, I experienced one of those life-changing moments: I began to see the patchwork of leaves as I had never seen them before. The small leaf in my hand, while very beautiful and unique in itself, was part of something larger: a mosaic, a grand collage of many colors and shapes, a collage put together by the hand of the Master.

As I returned to my spot on the porch and began reflecting on God's design, another beautiful mosaic came to mind, the mosaic of small groups that had grown over the years at Asbury United Methodist Church in Tulsa, Oklahoma. It occurred to me that although all maple leaves are similar in shape and size, they are quite different from oak leaves. And just like the mosaic of leaves that lay before me, the small groups, with all their similarities and differences, form another kind of grand collage put together by the Master's hand.

Asbury United Methodist Church, with a present membership of nearly six thousand, didn't set out from the beginning to develop a *mosaic* of small groups. The mosaic was the natural outcome of a core value that encouraged individuals to remain unique while developing meaningful relationships through small-group participation.

Asbury was founded in the 1960s as a traditional neighborhood congregation. For a few years, it was easy for its members to receive nurture from a single pastor and to develop meaningful relationships through a small array of Sunday school classes. As the congregation grew, however, small groups became essential for relationship building and meeting the ministry needs of a diversity of people.

In an effort to enrich the community life, leaders at Asbury began sponsoring a handful of small groups. Some were definitely more successful than others. After several tries, however, a pattern began to emerge. A group would flourish for a while and then wane or die out altogether. Before long, another group would come to life and typically repeat the same pattern. Some groups met without official knowledge or support of the church. Others developed on their own, completely outside of church support. On one occasion, a small home-fellowship group started by lay leaders was intentionally *disbanded* because it was different from the more highly structured groups that were developed by the staff. For all intents and purposes, early attempts at small-group ministry were unsuccessful.

Some Reasons Early Small-Group Efforts Were Unsuccessful

After assessing Asbury's early efforts to launch a successful small-group ministry, several areas were identified as problematic:

- lack of variety in the groups,
- lack of experience with small groups,
- unreasonable time commitments for participants, leaders, and facilitators, and
- shortage of appropriate and interesting study materials.

Although rare, other problems included (1) basic incompatibility and personality differences between the leader and group members, (2) different expectations between the leader and group members (such as leaders who wanted to lecture while members wanted to discuss), and (3) group members who were so diverse that they had no common interests.

As Asbury struggled to find the perfect model for small groups, it eventually discovered there was no such thing. Just as God provides variety in nature, a successful small-group ministry must do the same.

So, although Asbury had a rough beginning in small-group ministry, the outcome was a life-changing lesson. As Asbury struggled to find the perfect model for small groups, it eventually discovered there was no such thing. Just as God provides variety in nature, a successful small-group ministry must do the same. Why? Because there is no perfect small-group model that will meet the needs of everyone.

A mosaic approach to small-group ministry is one

that intentionally allows a variety of approaches to exist within the same congregation. In fact, many small-group ministries are unsuccessful simply because leaders try to pigeonhole groups into a single model.

Many small-group ministries are un-successful simply because leaders try to funnel all the groups into a single model.

If your congregation is typical, it is already a grand collage of many colors, shapes, and sizes. Your congregation is already a mosaic, crafted by the hand of the Master. The question is, Does your small-group ministry reflect it?

Essential Elements of Small-Group Ministry

Even in a mosaic approach, there are some common elements that most healthy small-group ministries have in common. Whether you are just beginning to develop a small-group program or are seeking to put new life into an existing one, the following elements will provide an essential starting place.

• The most important place to begin when starting or reviving a small-group program is in *prayer.* Start by praying that God will give you a vision for small groups. This vision must include the makeup of the initial leadership or design team, the shapes of the initial groups, and last but not least, the right timing. Pray that the leadership team will be committed to the vision and will work in harmony as it brings a diversity of spiritual gifts and personalities to the process. At

If your congregation is typical, it is already a grand collage of many colors, shapes, and sizes. Your congregation is already a mosaic, crafted by the hand of the Master. The question is, Does your small-group ministry reflect it?

every team meeting, be sure to allow plenty of time for listening prayer or waiting on the Lord. A commitment to wait until there is team agreement is a smart investment in ensuring a healthy, enduring small-group ministry.

• A second key to success is gaining support of the senior pastor. A lack of support from the top or executive level will decrease the chances for a successful small-group ministry. This key cannot be overstated. If

It is absolutely vital for the senior pastor to be fully committed to small groups as a basic strategy for ministry.

the pastor is not *on board,* those who want a vital small-groups ministry may as well invest their time elsewhere. Successful small-group programs are typically found in congregations whose senior pastor has a vision for the life-changing importance of small groups. The most effective place for the pastor to share his or her encouragement is both from the pulpit and in personal contact with individual members of the congregation. It is absolutely vital for the senior pastor to be fully committed to small groups as a basic strategy for ministry.

• The third key to success in a small-group ministry resides in the leadership team. In any sizeable congregation, the work of developing small groups can't be left to the senior pastor alone. Thus, one of the early steps is the prayerful development of a leadership team. Actually, this team will probably be one of the first intentional mosaics you put together. It should be a cross-sectional representation of the congregation itself.

A vital role for any ministry team is working closely with pastoral leadership. At Asbury, while the senior pastor is committed to small-group ministry, he functions more as a consultant than an actual team member. The team itself is given freedom to experiment and to discern God's will. The pastor continues to be supportive but demonstrates his trust in the team by allowing God to work through it. This trust and freedom to experiment continue to make a lot of difference in a thriving and growing small-group program.

This issue of trust and freedom, however, brings up another matter that can have a significant impact on the health of a small-group ministry: *control.* It is difficult for anything to grow in a healthy manner if it is constantly in the shadow of a controlling person or group. There is a space that exists between control and neglect. The more we acknowledge this space and seek to live within it, the more fruitful the small-group ministry will be.

There is no way we as humans could have planned the mosaic of small groups that has emerged at Asbury as a result of prayer, pastoral support, and a diverse leadership team. But what's even more wonderful than seeing the beautiful leaves falling one by one in my yard is watching God continue to bless our small-group ministry *one leaf at a time*. To our delight, God's mosaic continues to change and grow.

Group Design

For purposes of understanding and organization, groups most often fall into one of two primary designs: *accountability groups* and *home-fellowship groups*.

Accountability groups

Accountability groups typically consist of four or five members of the same sex. Just as its name implies, this group design is based on an element of accountability or covenantal relationship. The format of this group typically involves the members each sharing with the others how they have been accountable to the covenant of the group. A *covenant* is a simple statement, or promise, of things that all the group members agree to hold themselves accountable for. Areas of accountability include prayer, Bible study, faithfulness, honesty, and anything else the group includes in its covenant. Because accountability groups are somewhat autonomous, there is typically little in the way of oversight. Depending on the maturity and commitment of the leaders, this can be either a strength or weakness of the system.

To be successful, accountability groups require the following:

• **teaching** from the pulpit that reinforces the necessity of Christians to be held accountable to God and one another,

• **a leader** whose primary task is to facilitate each meeting,

• **a covenant** that is usually constructed by the members of each group, and

• **follow-up** to assess how the groups are doing and to provide additional resource assistance.

Training for accountability group leaders typically begins with teaching them the meaning of a covenant. Other essential areas of

It is difficult for anything to grow in a healthy manner if it is constantly in the shadow of a controlling person or group.

leadership training include inviting members to join and following up with those having difficulty remaining faithful to the group's covenant. Since accountability groups are not intended primarily as study, fellowship, or outreach groups, only minimal leadership training is typically provided. Accountability groups will often pass around the leadership role, having a different person start the group process at each meeting.

The primary value of these groups is the development of spiritual disciplines in the lives of the members. The challenge for members of these groups is in maintaining motivation to meet after the excitement of the covenantal promises wane. Success comes from encouraging one another to remain faithful to the covenant and to God.

The following covenant provides an example of those used by many accountability groups.

Accountability Group Covenant

I acknowledge God's grace as given through his son Jesus Christ (John 3:16), and in grateful appreciation, I will pledge myself to be his disciple. Thus, I make this covenant:

General Commitment to the Group

- I will meet each [weekday] from [start time] to [finish time] with my group.
- I will miss a meeting only when I have a reason of which I know God would approve.
- I will notify another member of the group if I will be unable to attend.
- Honesty and confidentiality will be of utmost priority. What is shared inside the group will be held in complete confidence.

Commitment to God

I pledge myself to

- daily devotions and study,
- daily prayer for the others in the group,

- weekly Sunday school participation, and
- weekly participation in worship.

Commitment to Myself and Others

In addition, each week I will

- take care of myself physically and maintain physical fitness;
- be a faithful steward of all God's financial blessings in my life;
- balance my time between family, profession, and leisure;
- make certain my speech gives evidence of my Christian faith;
- control my anger and find healthy ways to release it; and
- respond to Jesus' "In as much as..." statement found in Matthew 25:34-45 by seeking to help someone every week.

Commitment to Purity and Faithfulness

I also commit myself to

- avoid persons, places, and things that I know have a potential to draw me into temptation,
- avoid dwelling on that which I know is wrong, and
- confess my sins as I become aware of them.

Personal, Short-Term Commitments

If I feel so led, I will make a specific, short-term covenant with the group that is not binding on them, but only on me. I expect the group members to hold me accountable to my commitment. (Share weekly.)

My signature indicates that I understand and, with God's grace and strength, seek to uphold this covenant.

Signature:_____ Date:_____

Home-Fellowship Groups

Home-fellowship groups typically take on any one of several labels, including care groups, sharing groups, *koinonia* groups, and growth groups. No matter what they are called, the primary design for these groups is basically the same. They meet in homes and have leaders who have been through some type of small-group training program. In

The most important place to begin when starting or reviving a small-group program is prayer. Start by praying that God will give you a vision for small groups.

addition, home-fellowship groups typically have ten to fourteen members who covenant with each other to attend meetings regularly and to be faithful to the life of the group. Home-fellowship groups can consist of married couples, singles, or a mixture of both, and with an age range just as diverse. These groups usually have a predetermined life span (anywhere from six months to two years), or they may last indefinitely.

Home-fellowship group meetings are usually one and a half to two hours in length and include some form of Bible study, prayer, sharing, and fellowship. Many of these groups are involved in some type of community ministry. Although each home-fellowship group has its own personality, each is typically linked to the church in some manner.

To be successful, home-fellowship groups require the following:

• **a facilitator** who has the gifts of compassion, understanding and leadership;

• **training** for leaders (both initial and ongoing);

• **intentional placement** of group members, even more so than in accountability groups;

• **study materials** appropriate to the needs of the group;

• **a leadership contract** between facilitators and church staff that details leader support and accountability;

• **follow-up** to assess how the groups are doing and whether or not additional resource assistance is desired; and

• **pastoral investment** in the value of small groups to the life of the church.

Learning From Asbury's Experiences

When Asbury decided to become intentional about its small-group ministry, an initial *design team* was put together. The team decided to start the program by first initiating *home-fellowship groups.* The team chose to call them *koinonia groups* since the pastor had recently presented a sermon series on the word *koinonia* and its primary meaning, *to belong.* Thus, our goal was to instill within each small group a strong sense of belonging, to give the members the sense of being a little church within the big church.

After developing the initial plan, the second task was to identify the first leaders and provide them the necessary training. As with any sizeable congregation, it was difficult to know exactly who had the right combination of gifts to be effective group leaders. Several options were available as we began searching for the initial

Our initial training for small-group leaders was fairly extensive. And it definitely paid off. It didn't take long to discover the substantial benefit of investing in small-group leadership training.

leaders: (1) We could have each member of the design team lead a group; (2) we could make use of a spiritual gifts database; or (3) we could put out a call through the church newsletter inviting all those interested to participate in the leadership training program. Our final decision was to use all three methods to recruit small-group leaders.

We definitely acknowledged the importance of each member of the design team becoming a leader in an effort to get firsthand experience in small-group life. So each of the design team members committed to lead a group. We didn't want to ask others to do what we were unwilling to do ourselves. Our efforts were quite successful as our first training class consisted of nearly twenty-five people.

Training and Support for Leaders

The initial leadership training program consisted of meeting together one evening a week for seven weeks. At the end of that time, trainers met privately with each potential leader to confirm whether he or she still sensed a call from God to serve in this area. Our initial training for small-group leaders was fairly extensive. And it definitely paid off. It didn't take long to discover the substantial benefit of investing in small-group leadership training.

As a result of our experience, we identified several elements as vital to the training process. Here are a few of the most important:

The biblical basis for small-group ministry. An important part of the training process is in helping leaders understand that small-group ministry was Jesus' primary model of teaching others. He demonstrated this through his relationship with the disciples. Jesus' group was an ongoing learning lab in which the disciples learned from his words and actions and then applied what they learned in their own lives. What better reason can there be for small-group discipleship than that it was the way that Jesus invested so much of his ministry?

Styles of leadership. It is important for group leaders to identify and understand their own leadership styles and to recognize how each one affects group dynamics. Because people respond differently to different leadership styles, successful leadership training resides in leaders having knowledge of their own spiritual gifts and being able to make necessary adjustments based on personalities and needs within the group.

Relationships in the group. A training program should include basic things, such as the components of a balanced meeting, how to lead a meeting, and how to get others involved. In addition, leaders need to learn how to be sensitive to the needs of group participants. Sometimes a planned study is best put aside while group members listen and provide comfort to someone who is hurting. This segment of the training program should include a list of available counseling resources as well as training to know when a member should be referred for outside help.

Communication in the group. Most potential leaders have fairly well-developed communication skills. It is always helpful, however, to review both verbal and nonverbal communication, especially listening skills. Many leaders are more comfortable with speaking than listening and need to practice listening.

Faith sharing in the group. A vital part of the training process is in helping leaders learn to share their own faith journeys. The importance of allowing time in a group meeting for members to talk about how God is working in their lives cannot be overemphasized.

Choosing study materials. Some churches solve the problem of study material selection by developing their own curriculum. Other churches use materials published by a particular denomination or publishing house. Being locked into a single type of resource, however, results in a group missing out on many wonderful studies available from a wider variety of publishers. The training process should expose leaders to a wide variety of materials.

This is also a good training segment to introduce potential leaders to the different styles of learning. Some people learn visually, some audibly, and others through touch. It's important for leaders to employ a variety of learning styles and activities to make the group experience more meaningful.

> *An important part of the training process is to help leaders understand that small-group ministry was Jesus' primary model of teaching others...Jesus' group was an ongoing learning lab in which the disciples learned from his words and actions.*

Continued training and support for group leaders. Ongoing training and support of leaders is a vital part of effective small-group ministry. It is especially important to recognize and affirm their gifts of leadership on a regular basis. In addition, leadership meetings should be held at least bimonthly to provide opportunities for skill building, sharing innovative ideas, and praying for one another. Another worthwhile investment is to hold a yearly one-day retreat for team building, skill building, and fellowship opportunities.

Coaches—a key to leadership support. In my role as small-groups director, I initially resisted the idea of using coaches. It seemed they would only add another level of unnecessary bureaucracy. What I discovered, however, was that once the number of groups began to grow, it was next to impossible for one person to provide support for all the leaders. As a result, we incorporated the idea of using small-group coaches.

> *In my role as small-groups director, I initially resisted the idea of using coaches. It seemed they would only add another level of unnecessary bureaucracy. What I discovered, however, was that once the number of groups began to grow, it was next to impossible for one person to provide support for all the leaders.*

A coach is a person who acts as a mentor and serves as a point person for a specified group of small-group leaders. Coaches provide much-needed assistance by staying in close contact with small-group leaders and by providing encouragement. Coaches should be available to leaders as needed but should also commit to checking in with them at regular intervals.

Putting the First Groups Together

Once the initial leaders were trained and had made commitments to begin groups, the real fun started. Early in the process of developing a design for the first groups, we looked at several different options to connect leaders and members. Some of the ideas included encouraging leaders to recruit their own members, having the staff or the design team put the groups together, and holding a small-group fair. We finally settled on the idea of holding a small-group fair which proved to be fun, not too much work, and highly successful. Since we were using the koinonia concept for our first groups, we decided to call our small-group fair the Koinonia Konnection.

Early in the process of developing a design for the first groups, we looked at several different options to connect leaders and members...We finally settled on the idea of holding a small-group fair which proved to be fun, not too much work, and highly successful.

There were several elements that helped make our fair a huge success:

Publicity. We publicized the fair in every way possible, beginning with word of mouth. The small-group leaders became actively involved in inviting people to attend. Other methods included announcements from the pulpit and church newsletter articles.

Holding the fair following Sunday worship. This provided a perfect opportunity for worshipers to hang around and attend after the church services. The last thing the pastor did at each worship service was to invite the congregation to attend the fair.

A festive atmosphere. Our fair included decorations, balloons for the kids, and refreshments.

Handout information. Before the fair we prepared a handout with information about each potential group, including a map showing where each would meet. Since some members felt safer going to the church building than finding their way through the neighborhoods, particularly at night, we scheduled two groups to meet at the church. The church also provided better opportunities for participants with limited physical mobility.

Ideas that were also given consideration in putting groups together included connecting people through neighborhood groups, zip code groups, downtown or airport groups for those who could meet during the day, and subgroups formed out of larger groups such as Sunday school classes.

Leader stations. During the fair we stationed each leader in a different location with a large, easy-to-read sign. The sign included information such as when and where the group would meet as well as information about their first study focus. Each leader was also given a sign-up sheet. One of the challenges for the leaders was to stop adding names to their list once it reached fourteen members. It was important for us to keep the groups truly *small groups*.

Life Stages of Small Groups

Not long after the koinonia groups started meeting, we discovered there were problems that needed attention. Just as some of the groups sailed along beautifully, others struggled, even to the point of one ending after meeting only six times. What we discovered in our attempts to identify some of the problem areas was that most small groups go through life stages. Each stage has unique challenges that must be understood and addressed for the group to move to the next stage and remain healthy.

These are the five primary life stages of a small group:
• Beginning
• Forming
• Challenging
• Functioning
• Releasing

What we discovered in our attempts to identify some of the problem areas was that most small groups go through life stages. Each stage has unique challenges that must be understood and addressed for the group to move to the next stage and remain healthy.

Beginning. This stage is identified as the time when the members of the group get to know each other at a superficial level. Group members traditionally develop a covenant and begin talking about their hopes for group participation. There is generally a sense of uncertainty about where the group is headed, so members look to the group leader for direction. If the leader doesn't provide strong leadership in this stage, the group will begin to flounder and some members will lose interest. The *beginning* stage can last a few weeks or several months. One of the primary benefits of this stage is that new members can be added fairly easily.

Forming. During this stage, most groups continue to need strong leadership and direction. This often creates an interesting dynamic because it is usually here where the leader begins wondering just how much leadership to provide and how much to allow from other group members. At this stage, participants usually begin to feel more comfortable with each other. Unfortunately, some groups never move from here because their focus remains inward and superficial. It is easy to become so interested in common social interests that personal growth never occurs. Adding new members to the group at this stage can sometimes be a bit unsettling, and success depends on how well the leader prepares for assimilation.

Challenging. This is the stage where differences among group participants become apparent. By now, members have observed differences in one another in areas such as faith commitment, knowledge of Scripture, individual lifestyle, levels of energy, and commitment to the group. These differences can often produce challenges to the group dynamic. If trust hasn't been intentionally developed by this stage, one of two courses can occur: Either members will depart when the relationships become risky, or they will close off to avoid becoming authentic. It is crucial at this stage for the leader to recognize this as a normal part of small-group dynamics and not be surprised if it occurs. The intensity of the challenge depends on the strength of personalities within the group. If some of the members have stronger personalities or leadership tendencies than the leader, the challenge is often intensified.

If this stage is prolonged, it could disrupt the life of the group. Depending on its severity, outside intervention may be necessary. This stage is not the time to bring new members into the group.

Functioning. In this stage, members are consciously aware of a mutual commitment to stay together as a group and remain loyal to the group covenant, and they are learning to support rather than change one another. It is here that members become close and learn to trust one another. By now, the leadership is typically shared, and the power games from the previous stage have been resolved. The group begins to look outward toward a service ministry of some type. The length of this stage varies with each group. A healthy group may remain together for one year or ten years. For the group to remain healthy, it must stay committed to a balance of study, prayer, fellowship, and service beyond itself. It is also important in this stage to discuss how to handle changes in the group. Any long-term group should expect members to leave through attrition. If a group fails to make provisions to add new members, there is potential for extinction. A group that has made it to this stage should be able to handle the addition of new members. The biggest challenge will be to make new members feel as though they are a significant part of the group.

Releasing. Most long-term small groups will see members come and go. Also, leaders occasionally move on and leave the group in the hands of other members. Sometimes group members leave after developing a sense of accomplishing everything they can from the group; some leave because of unresolved conflict.

Small groups are like people: They all have a span of life that ends at some point. One of the most meaningful things a leader can do is help the group end gracefully. Hopefully it will be an end that is both prayerful and intentional. Since members have invested a significant part of their lives in long-term groups, they need time to say goodbye. They need time to cherish together what God has done through the group. A time of special blessing for one another and a group picture are

Small groups are like people: They all have a span of life that ends at some point. One of the most meaningful things a leader can do is help the group end gracefully.

very appropriate and will leave members with wonderful memories.

There are three primary signals that a group may be nearing the releasing stage:

• Several members seem restless or irregular in attendance;

• There is listlessness in the study and sharing; or

• The leader lacks enthusiasm.

When the leader has *any* sense that a group is nearing the releasing stage, it is unwise to consider adding new members.

Adding New Members to a Group

One of the great values of bringing new people into a group is the new life perspective each brings. New members will help keep a group fresh and growing. From the inception of a group, the leader should set the tone in regard to adding new members. Generally, adding one person or a couple at a time is easier than adding several all at once. Each new member needs an adequate opportunity to become assimilated. It should generally be the responsibility of the leader to talk with the group about inviting additional people to attend meetings. Most groups will readily accept guests as long as the leader and host expect them. Adding new members should always be discussed with the group in advance, no matter how open and accepting the group may be.

A Mosaic of Groups

That beautiful maple tree in my yard provides a great sense of enjoyment for me. Unfortunately, it does little to include variety in my vision. However, as its red leaves mix with the yellow, brown, and orange, a mosaic is formed, a mosaic that is ever changing!

Small groups, by their own unique forms, can develop into similar mosaics. Since variety is the central defining characteristic of a mosaic, to speak of a small-group mosaic is to imply the existence of variety and diversity. Lack of diversity in a small-group ministry can be the primary reason that it fails to flourish. As I mentioned earlier, groups generally fall into one of two primary designs, *accountability groups* and *home-fellowship groups*. However, there is a variety of ways to pattern small groups within these designs. The pattern is determined primarily by the need of the group and its desired outcome. It is variety within the patterns that provides the primary colors to a small-group mosaic.

> *Since variety is the central defining characteristic of a mosaic, to speak of a small-group mosaic is to imply the existence of variety and diversity. Lack of diversity in a small-group ministry can be the primary reason that it fails to flourish.*

Turbo groups. Turbo groups often serve a dual purpose as both interactive and leadership-training groups. These groups are often designed to be short term and end when the participants are adequately trained to serve as group leaders. Participants are often asked to join this type of small group for the expressed purpose of learning how to function as leaders. A turbo group is essentially a learning lab. The downside of these groups, as we experienced at Asbury, was that members had such a wonderful group experience they didn't want to end after completing the eight-week training session. In one particular instance, a turbo group started their own group. They added several more people, and overall the group has been a great success. The group didn't fulfill its original purpose, but a mosaic approach to small groups must expect the unexpected and make the best out of every opportunity.

> *The group didn't fulfill its original purpose, but a mosaic approach to small groups must expect the unexpected and make the best out of every opportunity.*

Table talk groups. This style of group helps potential leaders test the waters before they commit to more training. The group sessions are traditionally made up of two segments. The first segment consists of a large-group presentation or lecture with little opportunity for discussion. After the presentation, participants move to round tables. Once in the smaller groups, the leader, who has been designated in advance, takes the group through a discussion of the presented material. The discussion often includes time for both sharing and prayer.

Table talk groups provide an excellent opportunity for potential leaders to facilitate a group in a controlled environment. Turbo groups can also serve as dynamic small discipleship groups.

New believers' groups. These groups provide a significant opportunity for evangelism and discipleship within a congregation. If a congregation is actively involved in the discipleship of new believers, the groups will provide ideal settings in which participants can learn, grow, and discover their gifts of ministry. The leaders of new-believers' groups must be mature Christians who are flexible and have the capacity to respond to difficult questions. This type of group is definitely not the place for a *leaderless* group.

Ministry-related groups. Those who work together in a common ministry generally form these groups. Examples of ministry-related groups include choirs, orchestras, worship teams, puppet and drama teams, and teaching teams. The basic idea is for these groups to meet for rehearsal and, afterwards, study, support, and prayer.

Mission groups. Members of these groups share a passion for those outside the walls of the church. Mission groups may come together for a short term, such as a mission trip, or they may be involved in an ongoing service ministry. Either way, one of the components of this type of group is to develop community together through a mutual sense of mission.

Service groups. Groups of this type come together to provide opportunities for ministry in such areas as Meals on Wheels, Habitat for Humanity, straightening the pew racks, food service, or room setup. These groups may meet weekly or only one or two times a year. Members of service groups can be transformed into fruitful small groups if they are encouraged to seek opportunities for prayer, sharing, and study together.

Small groups for teens and children. These groups provide an excellent way for children and teenagers to comfortably enter a new church when they are unfamiliar with others in their age group. Most kids and teens find it easier to enter a group of five to eight than a large group. The focus for the group leader is to provide opportunities and smooth the way for participants to become part of the larger body.

Asbury has recently started what we call Kids Konnection groups. These are for fourth- and fifth-graders who meet weekly after school for a period of six weeks. Kids learn Scripture as well as how to listen and pray for each other.

Support groups. These groups are definitely vital for a small-group mosaic. They include such things as divorce recovery, employment assistance, mental health, cancer support, and so forth.

Intergenerational groups. These groups typically involve whole families. The basic group focus is to provide a combination of family time, encouragement, and developing bonds with other families. Intergenerational groups may spend the entire meeting together or spend only part of it together and then break into smaller groups for age-specific activities. This is an excellent approach to small groups that involves single-parent families or a mixture of single and two-parent families.

Men's and women's accountability groups. Accountability groups were discussed earlier but are worth mentioning again because of their importance to the small-group mosaic. These groups are typically small and can meet almost anywhere and at any time.

At Asbury, men's accountability groups have been very successful. They grew as a natural extension to the men's Wednesday morning prayer breakfasts. The pastor responsible for men's ministry works with a lay coordinator to get as many men involved in accountability groups as possible. At almost any time of day, you will find small groups of men gathered at the church to pray, to encourage one another, and to hold each other accountable to their group covenant.

A vital part of the small-group mosaic is to sense where God is working in the life of the congregation and to respond.

Ideas for organizing small groups can go on and on and are limited only by a congregation's creativity and resources. Wherever and whenever there is a need, a small group can be put together. A vital part of the small-group mosaic is to sense where God is working in the life of the congregation and to respond.

Other Issues Relating to a Healthy Small-Group Ministry

Child care is a very important issue in a fruitful small-group ministry. Parents should be encouraged to belong to groups, but without child-care resources, they may decline involvement. Possibilities for care include everything from letting parents work out their own arrangements to hiring a caregiver for all the children of a group at a central home to providing child care at the church. Of all the possibilities, child care provided at the church has been the most successful at Asbury. By providing it at the church, parents can depend on consistent, high-quality care.

If the decision is made to provide small-group child care at the church, the church may choose either to underwrite the expense or to ask parents to help with the cost. The children's ministry council or other governing body should develop guidelines for small-group child care.

Keeping track of groups and their members is quite time consuming and often a thankless job. However, it is important if a church is going to be intentional about involving as many people in small groups as possible. Tracking provides an effective way to measure success. When a small-group ministry begins, even in a large congregation, it is easy to know who the leaders are, who is in what group, when they meet, what they are studying, and what their mission project is. One person can track ten or fifteen groups fairly easily. Computer databases provide an excellent way to keep up with the groups, even if it simply lists group leaders, participants, and when they meet.

Growing and developing additional groups are simultaneously the delight and challenge of every church that is serious about small-group ministry. Often the first groups will fill up quickly, and then a waiting list will develop. Turbo and table talk groups provide effective ways to identify potential new leaders and start new groups.

Some small-group ministries begin new groups by increasing the size of a group and then dividing it into two groups. The key to this strategy is to have leaders identify an apprentice, or assistant, within their group. When the need for a new group arises, the original leader continues with part of the group, while the apprentice leads the other part of the group. Each group then intentionally works at adding new members. This is a very effective way to multiply groups in a congregation.

At Asbury we have found a slightly altered version to be most effective. Rather than dividing the current group, we leave it intact except for the leader, who moves to a new group and leaves the initial group in the hands of the apprentice. Groups seem to handle the loss of one member much easier than losing a large portion of their group.

What about those who aren't in a group? How can we make sure they receive care? One solution is to prepare small groups to be caregivers and intentionally connect them with individuals not in a group. It is best to limit the number to three or four nonmembers per group. Members then have the opportunity to provide ministry to those not in a group by inviting them to meetings and church socials, sending birthday and anniversary cards, and visiting them when they are sick or in need. This is an effective way to recruit new group members and stay attuned to the needs of those not in a group.

Leader retirement is an issue almost all groups have to face at one point or another. Even the most faithful leaders have a desire to retire eventually. Ideally, either the small-group staff person or a member of the leadership team will do an exit interview with the retiring leader. The purpose of the interview is twofold: (1) to thank the leader for many hours of leadership and ministry and (2) to learn from the leader how to make improvements in the small-group ministry of the church. Small-group leaders are an important asset and should not only be listened to and taken seriously but should be given the same care they have provided for others.

Suggested Small-Group Resources

Barker, Steve, and Ron Nicholas. *Good Things Come in Small Groups*. Downers Grove, IL : InterVarsity Press, 1985.

Bunch, Cindy, ed. *Small Group Idea Book: Resources to Enrich Community, Worship, Prayer, Nurture, Outreach*. Downers Grove, IL: InterVarsity Press, 1996.

Corrigan, Thom. *Fitness Kit: How to Keep Your Group Healthy and Growing*. Colorado Springs, CO: NavPress, 1996.

Davis, Deena, ed. *Discipleship Journal's 101 Best Small Group Ideas*. Colorado Springs, CO: NavPress, 1996.

Hamlin, Judy. *The Small Group Leaders Training Course: Everything You Need to Organize & Launch a Successful Small Group Ministry in Your Church, Training Manual*. Colorado Springs, CO: NavPress, 1990.

Long, Jimmy, ed. *Small Group Leaders' Handbook, the Next Generation*. Downers Grove, IL: InterVarsity Press, 1995.

McBride, Neal F. *How to Build a Small-Groups Ministry*. Colorado Springs, CO: Nav-Press, 1995.

McBride, Neal F. *How to Lead Small Groups*. Colorado Springs, CO: NavPress, 1990.

Sheeley, Steve. *Ice Breakers and Heart Warmers*. Littleton, CO: Serendipity House, 1996.

CHAPTER 2

Small Groups in Servant Ministry

PAUL BORTHWICK

Paul Borthwick serves as a mobilizer for world missions by teaching, writing, and speaking. He is currently Lecturer in Missions at Gordon College in Wenham, Massachusetts, and a staff member of Development Associates International.

What Can I Do to Breathe New Life Into This Group?

Phil's small group had been meeting for eight months. Then they developed a problem: They became ingrown. People complained that the meetings were too negative. It seemed as though everyone was focusing on his or her own problems. Phil began to notice an increase in selfishness, exaggeration of minor struggles, and occasional infighting.

In an effort to keep the small group from derailing, Phil came to me and asked, "What can I do to breathe new life into this group?" I immediately suggested service—a mission—a purpose bigger than the group itself, one that would help the members contribute something valuable and give them a greater sense of growth.

> *Phil came to me and asked, "What can I do to breathe new life into this group?" I immediately suggested service—a mission—a purpose bigger than the group itself, one that would help the members contribute something valuable and give them a greater sense of growth.*

Most Christian leaders have at one time or another used the "Red Sea-Dead Sea" analogy. There are two bodies of water in the Middle East. The Red Sea is full of living and growing organisms, good for fishing, and alive. The Dead Sea is just the opposite; it is lifeless, full of minerals and, as its name implies, dead. What is the difference? Both have an input source, but only the Red Sea has output. The analogy comes from applying this illustration to the Christian life. If we want to be alive and vibrant, we need both input and output. Without both, we will simply stagnate from an accumulation of knowledge without application.

This truth applies very powerfully to small groups. All input without output leads to insularity and stagnation. Jesus implied this concept when he started his small group of disciples. Mark's Gospel tells us that he appointed twelve, that they should be with him (input), and that he should send them out to preach (output) (Mark 3:14). The disciples were recruited on a learning mission that included service. Later, seventy-two were recruited on a service mission that included learning

(Luke 10:1-24). In the book of Acts, learning and service are combined: People came together in house-churches (or what we might call cell groups) and combined worship, prayer, outreach, and service to the poor (Acts 2:42-47).

These two purposes for coming together and forming groups perhaps reflect the personalities of those involved. Some people definitely gravitate toward the more contemplative learning group. Others choose action and join groups dedicated to service. However, upon close examination, the biblical model combines the two approaches.

Small groups that turn inward and insular become stagnant pools that spawn friction and interpersonal strife. On the other end of the spectrum, small groups that abandon community in favor of service often produce burnout, frustration, and pseudocommunity...

Whether small-group facilitators are working with a single group or multiple groups, they face the challenge of building balance between service and community. Small groups that turn inward and insular become stagnant pools that spawn friction and interpersonal strife. On the other end of the spectrum, small groups that abandon community in favor of service often produce burnout, frustration, and pseudocommunity, where time spent in service eliminates the time given to care for each other.

The Bible affirms both: **Community plus mission equals changed lives.** The Scriptures exemplify this concept, especially through the examples of church ministry in the Book of Acts.

What's more, the Bible challenges us to embrace the concept of community and mission together as it teaches us to "look not only to your own interests, but also to the interests of others" (Philippians 2:4). Indeed, the Bible offers community plus service as a prescription for growth.

Two Models of Small Groups in Servant Ministry

Model 1: *Mission Follows Community*

Phil's small group identified the problem of their inwardness and decided to get involved in a monthly mission project. They began meeting three of four Sunday afternoons for sharing, prayer, a meal together, and Bible study. On the fourth Sunday, they traveled together into nearby Boston and volunteered their services by preparing and serving meals at an inner-city soup kitchen called Kingston House.

Phil's group initially came together for personal fellowship, but they decided in their growth journey to serve together by adopting a project for outreach. Their depth of experience as a community increased dramatically. In their case, their **mission followed community.**

In a Sunday school setting, members of an ongoing class for young married couples had one of the closest fellowship groups in the church, but they wanted more. One couple heard about an opportunity to serve young children in an orphanage in Haiti. The couple presented the opportunity, and three other couples joined them for ten days, serving, building, and feeding very poor children in Port-au-Prince, Haiti.

Even though the rest of the class didn't go on the mission trip, they got involved. They raised the money needed for the team and collected seventy duffel bags full of food and clothing for the orphanage. Together the class and the eight who traveled joined in a mission that was larger than their class and greater than their personal concerns. By working together and building on the group cohesiveness they had already established in the class, their **mission followed community.**

Dr. Ron Sider, author of *Rich Christians in an Age of Hunger,* recently began challenging existing small groups to undertake mission together by joining in a covenant he calls the "The Generous Christian Pledge" ("Take the Pledge," Christianity Today, September 7, 1998). Sider encourages small groups to undertake a lifestyle mission for the poor by pledging the following:

"I pledge to open my heart to God's call to care as much about the poor as the Bible does.

"Daily, to pray for the poor, beginning with the Generous Christians Prayer: Lord Jesus, teach my heart to share your love with the poor.

"Weekly, to minister, at least one hour, to a poor person: helping, serving, sharing with, and mostly, getting to know someone in need.

"Monthly, to study, at least one book, article, or film about the plight of the poor and hungry and discuss it with others.

"Yearly, to retreat, for a few hours before the Scriptures, to meditate on this one question: Is caring for the poor as important in my life as it is in the Bible?—and to examine my budget and priorities in light of it, asking God what changes he would like me to make in the use of my time, money, and influence."

Model 2: *Community Follows Mission*

Debbie heard that the church hoped to recruit a team to join with Habitat for Humanity in a five-home building project in a poor neighborhood in Boston. She knew how to hammer, loved to undertake projects that she could see to completion, and had two weeks of vacation saved up, so she signed up. Debbie joined a team that combined with other teams who worked intensely for two weeks of twenty-four-hour days (three shifts). They completed five new units that were dedicated later that summer.

When I asked Debbie if the experience was all she had expected, she replied, "Well, the hard work was just what I expected; what I didn't expect was how close I got with my co-workers. Although I was attracted to the task, I plan on signing up next year because of the friendships I built. I grew closer to my co-workers than I've ever been with anyone in my life. We've started a small group that will continue after the summer is over." For Debbie, **community followed mission.**

Grace Chapel in Lexington, Massachusetts, where I served as youth minister and later missions pastor, dedicates many people each summer to short-term work teams. They come together around a mission: painting, building, medical service, vacation Bible school, and evangelism. But the result is that they build community together.

Each summer, one of the most frequent comments from task-oriented mission team members sounds something like this: "This is the closest I've ever been with a group of people in my whole life."

These mission team workers reflect a huge movement across the country of short-term small groups that come together to serve others. Whether it is a small church that sends a team of six or a megachurch that recruits and sends hundreds, the thrust remains the same: The small-group community aspect of the project is secondary; their first goal is to get a job done. But living together, sharing in one another's lives for a short time, and working together toward a common goal builds a team. In their case, **community follows mission.**

Evaluating the Two Models

So which model is better? If we follow the biblical concept that "community plus mission equals changed lives," is one model superior to the other? Let's take time to examine how each approach individually has its own strengths and weaknesses.

Strengths of Model 1: *Mission Follows Community*

When an existing small group decides to undertake an ongoing mission project, the result is often a sense of deeper relationships with one another. As the small group endeavors to serve, participants become a team. They step out of a traditional small-group setting and begin to see one another in a new light.

The group that decided to serve monthly at the soup kitchen started to grow in ways that the safe environment of their small group had never allowed. They confronted each other's fears together. (Soup kitchens are not usually in the nicest section of the city.) They saw one another in varied states of weariness, impatience, and frustration. Getting outside the safe zone taught them more about unconditional love than a weekly small-group meeting ever could.

Ongoing service projects performed by existing community groups also create greater ability to build relationships and partnerships with the

When an existing small group decides to undertake an ongoing mission project, the result is most often a sense of deeper relationships with one another. As the small group endeavors to serve, participants become a team. They step out of a traditional small-group setting and begin to see each other in a new light.

people being served. For example, Sandra's small group adopted a ministry in the nearby city and served together faithfully for three years. The relationships Sandra built became the foundation for a job change. She joined the inner-city ministry, and a portion of her support came from her fellow small-group members.

Ben served as part of a college class small group that took three short-term missions to Uganda. The ongoing ministry with these leaders led him to a decision similar to Sandra's. The Ugandan leaders invited him to come and serve with them for two years because he had developed trust with them through his small-group mission work.

A third benefit of ongoing ministry performed by existing small groups is that it teaches faithfulness. Weekly or monthly service teaches people about the need for sustained ministry. One small group became involved in a tutoring program with disadvantaged kids and dedicated two nights a month to helping students with their homework. The object of their work was to keep these young people in school until they graduated. The ongoing, sometimes frustrating, oftentimes unsuccessful nature of their ministry taught them faithfulness. Eventually, the group attended the high school graduation of three of the students they had helped over a span of six years. Group members later commented, "It was an experience of the Lord saying to us, 'Well done, good and faithful servant.'"

A final strength of small groups involved in ongoing ministry relates to the effect that their service can have on other small groups (or in smaller churches, on the whole church). Their example inspires others. One small group adopted mentally ill children at a state hospital. They went to the hospital every Sunday before church and provided an hour of singing, hugging, and an occasional distribution of candy. They carried on that ministry for over twenty years. Their work set an example for others as it was featured in secular media as well as the church.

Weaknesses of Model 1: *Mission Follows Community*

An ongoing mission project carried out by existing small groups is not without its problems. Sometimes the unending nature of the ministry leads to frustration or boredom.

A college-age small group decided to use one of their four monthly meetings to visit lonely people at a local nursing home. The ministry went well for the first three months. However, by the fourth month, the group leader began to see an emerging pattern. Group members started missing "service week." They used a variety of excuses. When he dug deeper, the two primary reasons members cited were that they couldn't see progress and that it wasn't very rewarding."

Ongoing service through small groups can be boring. The service groups can also get sloppy and lose interest in those being served. The mundane routine of ministry can often make it tempting to concentrate more on serving each other or to pursue rewarding "perks" than to serve those in need.

One small group chose a yearly service project on the island of Trinidad. They chose to make the trip in the summer to make sure that they wouldn't be accused of making the trip as an excuse for escaping winter. But by the third summer, the leaders were forced to re-evaluate their mission. They began sensing that team members were going for fun, enjoyment, and the beach, rather than to serve and minister to the Trinidadians.

A final weakness of the small group going out in service occurs when members begin showing up for the experience of intimate fellowship rather than to serve. During one small-group mission trip that I led, we began experiencing some struggles with Del. We had been asked by a camp director to help build some brick walls. During the service activity, whenever I looked around, Del was off sitting in the grass, engaging in an in-depth conversation with another team member. When I confronted him, he retorted that he came to "minister to the group," which didn't really include chipping bricks and mixing cement.

Strengths of Model 2: *Community Follows Mission*

Gathering people into small groups for specialized service projects and creating the community as a result of the joint effort in the tasks

Perhaps the greatest strength of short-term mission service groups can be attributed to the measurable tasks that get accomplished. Team members learn the value of synergy created by a unified team. They learn that people working together can accomplish more than people working alone.

has its strengths and weaknesses as well.

Perhaps the greatest strength of short-term mission service groups can be attributed to the measurable tasks that get accomplished. Team members learn the value of synergy created by a unified team. They learn that people working together can accomplish more than people working alone.

Of course, an additional benefit is that of the team experience itself. Being thrown together with other team members provides indoctrination into teamwork and interdependency. It creates a community of necessity in those who might otherwise be task-oriented.

The church I referred to earlier, Grace Chapel, sits in a high-tech area and as might be expected, has many highly task-oriented engineers. They are attracted to short-term service projects that present a measurable, achievable task. Men and women join the team because they can actually see that their contributions make a difference. But the team's experience often provides an added surprise: They find themselves growing in meaningful relationships and a desire for continued community.

Another strength of the short-term community brought together for service comes from risk-taking faith. Team members find themselves forced to trust God together for things such as finances, safety, health, baggage-delivery, and more.

Teams sent out to serve act as catalysts in the church, no matter what the size. They inspire more short-term teams; they motivate people for long-term local service, as in the case of Sandra and Ben; and they create a hunger for deeper community relationships.

An additional benefit of short-term teams is the desire to repeat service trips to locations where they have built relationships with their hosts. Some short-term teams end up adopting long-term projects, either locally or in relationship to the people they served. One team that taught at an English-language evangelistic camp in Hungary joined to support a young Hungarian woman coming to the United States to study. Another team, consisting of teenagers who served with hearing-impaired people in Jamaica, returned home, held a signing class, and started a deaf ministry in their own youth group.

A final strength of short-term ministry teams is that participants receive a firsthand experience of community. Group members get to taste fellowship on a deeper level than they've ever experienced before. As a result, they acquire a hunger for true community.

Two years ago, an unusual blend of people came together for a ministry trip to serve prisoners and their families in El Salvador. The ethnically diverse group included a family of five and two divorcees, ranging in age from thirteen to fifty-four. What looked like an unlikely mix of people ended up bonding as a family. The last I heard of them, they were planning Thanksgiving Day dinner together. A group that came together based on a mission became a community.

Weaknesses of Model 2: *Community Follows Mission*

Short-term mission teams have their weaknesses as well. While they often create a temporary community on the service project, they do not guarantee the creation of an ongoing community or small group. Sometimes service teams actually return home and undermine the existing communities in other small groups.

Perhaps the greatest weakness stems from lack of proper follow-up or integration back into the larger existing fellowship. What do the participants do with this intense experience and the relationships that were built as a result?

Occasionally, teams that endure a tough mission project become cliquish. They take on an attitude that alienates people who are outside the group. This has the potential of being especially harmful in the tightknit fellowship of a small church. It sometimes takes the form of false spiritual superiority, such as, "We went to serve and you didn't." Other times it takes the form of community pride: "We've achieved a level of community that you've never experienced." Whatever form it takes, the result often discourages the church from seeing these mission projects as valuable. Facilitators have to work hard to help integrate teams back into the fellowship with practical "what-do-you-do-now" instructions.

At the opposite end of the spiritual clique, teams occasionally return home lonely because they can't duplicate the same intensity of community at home. As a result, they either forget the experience altogether, or they develop critical attitudes toward other small groups that do not achieve the same depth of commitment.

Pete struggled with this after he returned from an incredible experience with a team in Africa. The team disbanded, and Pete suffered extreme loneliness after returning because the intensity of "life together" could not be duplicated at home. He even struggled relating to his own wife. She wasn't able to go on the trip and hadn't experienced the depth of community that he had. He started comparing their married "community" to the intensity of fellowship he felt with his team. The result, of course, was a new tension between them. It took them several stressful weeks to work through the issues. The breakthrough came at the team reunion. Pete's wife was able to discern that all of the group members were experiencing the same feelings of loneliness because nothing back home duplicated what they had experienced in Africa together.

The Optimum Solution

What then is the best approach, given both the strengths and weaknesses of service that emanates out of existing small groups versus service teams that come together around a task?

The optimum approach to small-group ministry is to provide short-term mission experiences to feed long-term small-group relationships.

The optimum approach to small-group ministry provides short-term mission experiences to feed long-term small-group relationships. Such a plan creates a cycle as illustrated by the following diagram:

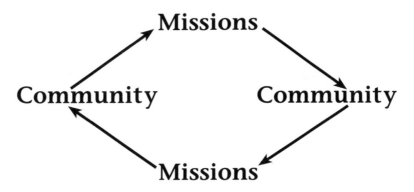

People may enter the cycle at any point. Some will desire the fellowship and intimacy of community, and they will be drawn into service. Others will be attracted to the idea of accomplishing tasks or engaging in service, and in that context, they will be drawn into community.

Maximizing Growth in Small-Group Servant Ministry

Whether you're engaged with the outreach ministry of ongoing small groups or sending out short-term mission teams, the following principles will help maximize relationship-building and service to others.

Training. As a youth pastor, I had the privilege of taking our young people through an intense program called Youth Evangelism Explosion. During the experience, I learned a valuable lesson: People grow and serve most effectively when they have been adequately trained.

This lesson has significant implications for both small groups and community-oriented service teams. Participants must be trained and prepared in advance for what they'll experience in each of three areas:

1. the actual ministry and work in which they will engage;

2. understanding the people they're serving; and

3. the team dynamics they'll experience.

On a recent ministry trip to Cuba, I learned the importance of training and preparation firsthand. A service group was waiting in a hotel lobby for a trip to a hospital. They were obviously part of a medical mission. Their behavior definitely revealed that they had been put together with little preparation as an ad hoc team to serve in health care. As they waited, a few of them rudely protested to the hotel staff that their van was late, and they began making comments about Cuban society as a whole. One member of the team sat on a couch in the lobby, visibly ill and afraid. Some reached out to her, but others disregarded her, as a potential hindrance to the team mission. The team undoubtedly had tremendous expertise in the health profession, but they obviously lacked training for the culture, the Cuban people, and for teamwork.

Obviously, training will vary with the nature of the service group. For example, the group I mentioned that serves every month at a soup kitchen might not need training in teamwork. They already meet at other times of the month where the group has developed its own team dynamics. On the other hand, they do need training to understand the sociology of homelessness. As a result of their training need, the group received training from the soup kitchen director to help them understand the people they were serving. In several short meetings with the team, he explained the causes of homelessness. As a result, the time spent in training increased the group's compassion for the people they serve.

After more than twenty years of sending out mission groups, ranging in age from young teenagers to senior adults, we developed a training regime that includes team meetings, team-building exercises, a team retreat, and a training manual. The goal of each area is to answer certain questions before a team goes out to serve.

The following framework provides a basic outline that can be adapted and used to train small groups involved in almost any type of servant ministry.

Concerning the work or ministry to be accomplished:
  • Does the team know what is expected of them?
  • Have they been adequately trained in the ministry being performed?

• Do they have the skills needed for the physical tasks that lie ahead?

• Do they have an understanding of the work ethic of the ministry leaders they're assisting?

• Will they have adequate supplies with them when they go?

Concerning the people (and culture) being served:

• Has the team been trained in cultural sensitivity? Do they know the difference between things being "culturally different" versus "wrong"?

• Do they have some understanding of the language they'll be working in?

• Do they understand the values and attitudes of the people they're serving with respect to potentially volatile cultural issues, such as modest attire, the role of women, styles of worship, or legalistic issues of Christian behavior?

• Has the team been briefed on things that can be difficult areas of adjustment, such as differences in food, hygiene, or health care?

Concerning team dynamics:

• Has the team been trained in handling conflict?

• Are there defined leaders of the team for the times when a group decision is not possible?

• Have people been oriented on key team-dynamic issues, like patience, encouraging each other, and asking and granting forgiveness?

• Does the team understand that teamwork takes priority over individual achievement?

Training makes or breaks a group's ability to experience maximum growth in service and community. People grow most and serve most effectively when they're adequately trained.

Covenantal relationships. The conflicts that exist in groups seeking to serve together usually result from errant expectations. Small groups in servant ministry will maximize their growth and service potential if they articulate and define goals that pertain to their

*Small groups in ser-
vant ministry will
maximize their growth
and service potential if
they articulate and de-
fine goals that pertain
to their work, their
team relationships, and
their tactics in conflict
resolution.*

work, their team relationships, and their tactics in conflict resolution.

One of the most effective ways to inform group members about expectations is through a small-group covenant. When a team creates a small-group covenant, they avoid many difficulties by defining how the team will work.

On one of our small-group mission teams, a member asked, "Why do we need to define the relationships? Shouldn't we just trust each other?" He saw the covenant as sort of prenuptial agreement between people trying to protect themselves. Instead, the covenant is more like a vow of marriage where we state to each other that we will be faithful to each other "through every change of condition." The team covenant defines the team vision, the interpersonal relationships, the tools for building team camaraderie, and the methods for both conflict resolution and relational evaluation.

The following covenant from a team that my wife and I led to Kenya several years ago illustrates the intention of such a stated agreement.

Sample Covenant: The Kenya Team

We, the members of the Grace Chapel Mission Team to Kijabe, Kenya, believing that God has called us together to serve, agree together concerning the following:

I. Our Vision

We desire our team to be characterized by Christlike behavior exhibited through unconditional love, unselfish service, and unified teamwork. Our ultimate purpose as a team and as individuals is in accordance with I Corinthians 9:23.

II. Our Team Objectives

We believe that we can fulfill this vision through the following commitments to each other:

A. *Teamwork:* We commit ourselves to be a group of individuals who unite as one, striving to accomplish the same goal: glorifying Christ and increasing his church.

B. *Communication:* We commit ourselves to resolve all intrateam conflicts according to biblical principles. This involves prayer as the first step, personal confrontation as the next step, and the counsel of a third party (namely, a leader) as a third and final resort. In all issues of conflict, we commit ourselves to maintain a humble spirit of confidentiality and seek to obey Ephesians 4:29.

C. *Forgiveness:* We commit ourselves to the recognition of sin as our common enemy so that we may each be sensitive to our human failings and forgive each other. We recognize that forgiveness is manifested through an understanding, forgetful attitude and the continuation of demonstrated love. In accordance with Hebrews 12:15, we commit ourselves to resolving any bitterness, because we realize that the bitterness will drag the whole team down.

D. *Spiritual growth:* We commit ourselves to personal worship and fellowship with God through obedience to the Lordship of Jesus Christ and an openness to learn from God's Spirit in all situations. We agree to have the same attitude as Paul the Apostle with respect to failure (Philippians 3:12-14) and with respect to perseverance (I Corinthians 9:24-27).

III. Our Team Structure

We believe that the following structural elements will enable us to carry out our team objectives:

A. *Team meetings:* Before, during, and after the project, our team meetings will be a crucial part of fulfilling the agreement of this covenant. These team meetings shall include team devotions, team prayer, time for communicating details and plans, and time for individual relational development.

B. *Personal quiet time:* We will all attempt to be as faithful as possible in our daily time with God because we believe that growing individually is essential to growing as a team.

C. *Affirmations:* We commit ourselves to the sending of daily notes of encouragement to one another throughout the duration of our project. These notes shall be sent according to a rotation of members so that each member must encourage (at one time or another) every other member several times.

D. *Ministry opportunities:* We will seek to be a witness to the love of

Jesus for the people we meet throughout our trip. This shall include testimonies, speaking in churches, and Christlike behavior. (See John 4:35.)

E. *Work:* We recognize that, if our objectives are to be completed, we must commit ourselves to work to the best of each of our God-given abilities every day. (See I Corinthians 10:31.)

F. *Prayer:* We commit ourselves to daily prayer for other team members using the following schedule:

- Monday: Paul & Christie
- Tuesday: Andy & Laura
- Wednesday: Elaina & Becky
- Thursday: Jeff & Glenn
- Friday: Jon & Jim
- Saturday: Kelly & Tom
- Sunday: Jared & Kirsten

G. *Leadership:* We recognize that Paul Borthwick is the official leader of our team, and that Christie Borthwick, Tom McLaughlin and Kirstin Wells are also team leaders. In situations of team concern, these leaders will be the team guides. We also recognize that the Kenya team is an opportunity for each of us to develop God-given leadership ability, and we commit ourselves to that end through the pursuing of individual growth opportunities that may arise.

IV. Evaluation/Accountability

We shall hold one another accountable to this covenant, and we shall measure our success in keeping this covenant by

A. Correcting each other according to biblical and covenant principles. (See Colossians 1:28.)

B. Responding without defensiveness when we are corrected and believing that other team members have our best interest and the interest of the team in mind. (See Proverbs 27:5-6.)

C. Meeting as a team within one month after our return home to review the covenant and evaluate our performance as a group.

I, _____, as a member of the Kenya team, commit myself to this covenant to the best of my God-given ability.

Date:_____ Signed:_____

The key to a covenant's effectiveness lies with its implementation. One group wrote a beautiful covenant at a team training day but then never looked at it again. They found their covenant useless. In contrast, another team taped their covenants in their Bibles and reviewed them three times before their service project and then every third day during their trip. They exchanged signed copies with each other as a statement that "I'm inviting you to hold me accountable to this covenant." They discovered

One of the challenges for small groups involved in servant ministry is in keeping their priorities straight. It's quite easy to allow the challenge of serving others to overshadow the need for group members to be intimately involved in praise and worship.

that the covenant was their group's greatest relational preparation.

Servanthood. Small groups in service ministry maximize the growth potential of their experience by emphasizing a servant's heart. To get small-group momentum going, we ask participants to memorize Philippians 2:5-11 in an effort to model the sacrificial example of Jesus. In addition, group-training meetings emphasize themes such as "how to love people you don't like" and "how to serve and be served." The intent is to teach people two basic principles: (1) Love depends on action, not feelings; and (2) developing humility in service comes from allowing others to serve you. Jesus washed the feet of others, and he allowed others to wash his feet.

Worship. One of the challenges for small groups involved in servant ministry is in keeping their priorities straight. It's quite easy to allow the challenges of serving others to overshadow the need for group members to be intimately involved in praise and worship.

Like Martha in Luke 10:38-42, it's easy to get so caught up in serving that God gets pushed out. Small-group leaders must structure groups to allow the members' work *for* God to flow from their worship *of* God.

Perhaps the best example of keeping this perspective is Mother Theresa's Sisters of Charity in Calcutta, India. Faced with the staggering human need in a city where over one million

Participants are empowered when they are given opportunities to use their talents.

live as homeless people in abject poverty, the sisters stay empowered to minister by setting aside time every morning for personal and corporate worship. They know that strength to serve others comes from an intimate relationship with God.

In *Let the Nations Be Glad!* author John Piper urges his readers to keep their perspective by making worship their focus. His premise is that "Missions exists because worship doesn't" and that all service and missions must flow out of our worship of God. When motivated by worship, God leads us out to serve others so they in turn might worship.

Creative Ways to Integrate Servant Ministry Into Small Groups

Whether you're serving a large church with hundreds of individuals involved in small groups or simply leading a small church fellowship group, the following steps will help add new vitality to your small-group ministry.

• **Set a foundation for recruitment.**

Leadership sets the tone for service and mission. If your desire is to strengthen relationships within small groups through service, launch your efforts with a sermon series, a Sunday school class presentation, or a small-group leader training seminar using servanthood as the theme. If the pastor and other church leaders emphasize that giving to others is a normal expression of a Christian's love for God (I John 4:19-20), others are more likely to join in.

Small groups involved in servant ministry can take many shapes and forms. Getting involved in this kind of ministry could be as simple as a church elder or deacon leading a Saturday service project with fellow leaders or a youth pastor taking a small youth group on an evening mission project.

In the ministry to senior adults, my mother got recruited onto a service team at age sixty-seven. Another widow, sixty-nine years of age, came to her and challenged her to join her on a trip to Kenya.

My mother couldn't say no because her likely excuse, "I'm too old," was taken away by a woman two years her senior!

• Identify what's already happening.

If you are involved in a large church with many small groups, don't assume that none of them are involved in a servant ministry of some type already. Meet with the leaders of your existing small groups to find out which ones have already adopted service projects. Making this information public can encourage others to do the same.

One particular church surveyed existing small groups and found that about 30 percent of them already had adopted service ministries, another 20 percent desired one, and several groups asked for opportunities to go out on a two-week service team. By publicizing existing servant ministries and by helping other small groups get started, church leaders almost doubled the number of groups involved in service.

Don't be afraid to "paint targets around existing arrows." Servant ministries in which small groups are already involved will provide greater motivation than external ministries that you try to introduce.

• Organize a prayer walk.

Our young adult ministry engaged in a community project by distributing town resource books to every household. We encouraged our participants to pray for each household and to keep their eyes open for opportunities to serve. The prayer walk motivated one small group to undertake ministry to the poor and another one ministry to the elderly.

One particular group took church leaders on a prayer walk in the community. As a result, they discovered a large number of first-generation American neighbors. The walk resulted in the development of an "English-as-a-second-language" ministry as well as a "welcoming group" outreach to internationals. A community prayer walk can cast a vision for service and outreach to those in our own communities.

• Do a survey.

A survey of existing small groups designed to discover skills, interests, and willingness to serve can be a great first step in involvement in servant ministry. Participants are empowered when they are given opportunities to use their talents.

One small group had several men with skills in automotive repair. Their group leader challenged them to volunteer a Saturday morning servicing vehicles belonging to single moms and elderly people in the church. It had such a positive effect that the men started their own quarterly ministry. All it took was for the small-group leader to help them make a connection between their automotive skills and servant ministry.

• Develop a servant ministry list.

People love options. Building a list of service opportunities for ongoing small groups will help motivate people by giving them choices.

Recently, I had a vision of sending a service team to Cuba. The idea ended up falling flat because I presented it as a "done deal" rather than as an opportunity that a group could choose and shape themselves. I had the contacts, I had the excitement, and I was trying to recruit others to join in fulfilling *my* plans. The project didn't come to fruition because it was my vision instead of theirs. I prepared for the trip in isolation, and none of the small groups had a sense of ownership.

In contrast to this approach, Mary Ann Mitchener, minister of urban outreach at Grace Chapel, gives small groups multiple options that they can shape and make their own. Mary Ann heads a ministry called "Bridge Builders," whose primary purpose is to build bridges between urban and suburban Christians. She oversees partnership ministry to the homeless, urban tutoring, serving unwed mothers, and a host of other projects.

She and her servant team have designed a special "Bridge Builders" booklet that serves as a "Yellow Pages" for service options. Each page describes a ministry, the small-group or individual service options, the gifts and skills needed, the duration of service opportunities, and the appropriate contact persons. By furnishing small-group leaders with this booklet, Mary Ann has connected dozens of small groups with ongoing and short-term service relationships.

• **Help groups own the vision from the beginning.**

If your desire is for small youth teams to get involved in servant ministry, begin by meeting with the youth leaders and listening to their vision first. If single adults are your targets, begin by consulting the singles' group leaders. It's important to listen to the vision of other leaders prior to presenting any new idea.

After only limited success in getting small groups involved in servant ministry, I discovered I had been going about recruitment and vision casting wrong. Instead of planning for teams without consulting ministry leaders, I began meeting with ministry leaders nine to twelve months *before* teams were to be sent out. I'd listen to their ministry goals and dreams. By working with leaders and seeking to serve their vision, the commitment to servant ministry increased dramatically because the leaders owned the vision from the beginning.

• **Don't reinvent the wheel.**

Anyone who gets excited about small groups getting involved in servant ministry can easily fall into the trap of trying to accomplish too much too soon. One church's small-group ministry attempted to start their program by taking a group of ten youth to Kenya for six weeks. Another church's first attempt at servant ministry began by taking over thirty team members to Tijuana, Mexico.

Although both teams were successful on some level, the first came home overwhelmed by a project that had been bigger than they could fulfill. The second group returned satisfied that they had accomplished many tasks but were dissatisfied with the low level of community they had achieved.

It is far better to start small. If there's interest in mission service, the best place to begin is by assembling a short-term "test" group, whose members begin serving locally at a soup kitchen or another community ministry. It's far easier to start small and build slowly than to recover after falling flat under a huge load.

In our church's partnership with a church in Moldova (a former USSR country east of Romania), we started much too big. Our vision was to send a team made up of our church leaders to serve with their leadership. The team included the senior pastor, several elders, various other ministry leaders, and one "guide" who had been to Moldova twice before.

All of the team members had experience in small-group ministry, but most of them had been exposed only to leading task-oriented groups at home. They were unready for the intensity and challenge of a multicultural community. Only a few of the members had any experience in the poorer world. As a result, many of them experienced an overwhelming emotional shutdown before the team returned. We learned our lesson by biting off "more than we could chew"! We learned on subsequent teams to increase both the training and the ratio of experienced leaders.

• Learn from others.

A church that has a vision to implement servant ministry into their small groups need not reinvent the wheel. There are many churches and parachurch ministries who specialize in mission work. Churches just beginning to engage in this type of work should consider enlisting their help to establish, prepare, train and send out mission teams. Existing ministries such as Group Workcamps, STEM, and Adventures in Missions stand ready and willing to provide help. (See further resources at the end of this chapter.)

• Set the example.

Although we attempted too much with our leadership team that went to Moldova, it was successful on one very important level. It set a precedent and example of small-group servant ministry. By sending a group made up of church leaders, we provided a solid example of how small-group service teams can be a vital part of church life.

If church leadership says, by their own participation, "Join with us in the life-changing, community-building opportunity of service teams," other participants are more likely to follow. However, if leaders communicate a "do as we say, not as we do" attitude as it relates to service teams, many church members will fail to see the significance of small groups involved in mission.

A Final Note

If your small-group program needs new life breathed into it, the answer may be as simple as helping each group capture the vision for a purpose bigger than the group itself. A purpose such as this can be realized and will come to fruition as small groups become involved in servant ministry.

Some churches already have small groups involved in servant programs. If they too appear to be in need of new life, rather than starting something new or adding more programs, begin by evaluating them against the four principles presented in this chapter: training, covenantal relationships, servanthood, and worship. Without a proper balance in these areas, servant ministry groups may fall short of recognizing their ultimate objective.

In either case, a vital element for any small-group ministry resides in its participants contributing something of value through service. The sense of Christian growth and accomplishment that comes as a result will certainly be worth the effort.

**Additional Resources for Small Groups
Involved in Servant Ministry**

Written Resources
• Michael J. Anthony, ed. *The Short-Term Missions Boom: A Guide to International and Domestic Involvement.* (Baker Books, 1994).

This book is primarily a compendium of articles on short-term service by a host of experts. Articles include topics related to vision (like the priority of relationship building) and practical matters (like training and finances). Section III identifies "Mission Projects Close to Home" and includes many ideas for ongoing small-group service.

• Tim Gibson, Steve Hawthorne, Richard Krekel, Ken Moy, eds. *Stepping Out: A Guide to Short-Term Missions* (YWAM Publishing, 1992).

This resource consists of a compendium dedicated to making the most of short-term service experiences. Articles cover almost every practical detail that leaders will encounter, from training to service to follow-up.

• *The Short-Term Mission Handbook* (Berry Publishing, 701 Main Street, Evanston, IL 60202, 1992).

This resource consists of multiple short articles on service teams combined with the most comprehensive list of short-term mission opportunities available. This publication serves as the "Yellow Pages" of short-term possibilities.

Mission Conference

• The National Short-Term Missions Conference (P.O. Box 4706, Wheaton, IL 60189-4706).

This annual conference draws some of North America's most experienced short-term mission leaders, churches, and agencies. Workshops and tracks include themes related to community development like "Team Building," "Conflict Management," and "Spiritual Formation."

Agencies That Coordinate Short-Term Service Projects

• Adventures in Missions, 437 Brenau Ave., Gainesville, GA 30501.

This agency specializes in church-based short-term service teams. They originally targeted youth groups but have expanded into adult teams as well.

• Center for Student Missions, 27302 Calle Arroyo, San Juan Capistrano, CA 92675-2768.

This agency specializes in cross-cultural exposure trips for youth in the inner cities of Washington, DC; Los Angeles; Chicago; Toronto; and more.

• Group Workcamps, P.O. Box 481, Loveland, CO 80539-0481.

Group Workcamps serves as a "broker" for small groups whose churches want to serve through an agency that coordinates all of the details for service. Teams come, join with other teams from across the country, and serve a needy community through some variations of physical labor—building, painting, raking, and so on.

• STEM (Short-term Evangelical Missions) Ministries, 5637 Brooklyn Blvd., #102, Brooklyn Center, MN 55429.

STEM consists of experts in coordinating church-based teams in service across cultures. Team leaders work with STEM to design the service project, and STEM provides the training, administration, and team details in places like Trinidad. Roger Peterson, president of STEM, has completed a study on the impact of short-term missions on the participants: "Are Short-term Missions Worth the Time and Money?" This resource helps leaders maximize the long-term growth potential of service teams.

CHAPTER 3
Small Groups in an Intergenerational Context

GARY C. NEWTON

Dr. Gary Newton currently serves as Associate Professor and Director of the M.A. program in Educational Ministries at Huntington College, Huntington, Indiana. In addition, Gary has served as a pastor and small-group facilitator for the past thirteen years.

Life-Changing Experiences

Some of most enriching experiences I've had as a pastor and church leader have happened within the context of small groups made up of persons from different age groups, from young children to senior adults. Although developing intergenerational small groups may seem awkward at first, with a little time and work, they can offer some of the most powerful and life-changing experiences in the life of a congregation. Besides, many times those who are most resistant to intergenerational experiences, if given a chance, will become the strongest cheerleaders.

It didn't take very many years in ministry for me to recognize that traditional church programs don't encourage relationships and understanding among different age levels. Even sermons focused on strengthening the family and community never seem to reach far enough to actually change the patterns of communication among generations. [My own experiences have shown that the most effective way to change the way generations relate to one another is by creating active experiences that bring them together.]

My own experiences have shown that the most effective way to change the way generations relate to one another is by creating active experiences that bring them together.

The following three accounts will help illustrate this point.

While serving as pastor of Christian education and youth in a church in Lancaster County, Pennsylvania, I made my first attempt at combining various age groups and family units. Instead of providing a typical Wednesday night adult prayer meeting and age-appropriate classes, I decided to divide the congregation geographically and have them meet in homes as intergenerational family groups for the summer. This turned out to be quite a challenge: choosing and training leaders, writing curriculum, recruiting participants, and tracking the progress of each group. The story of the entire summer, however, can be told in the story of a young girl named Sally.

Sally came from a rough, non-Christian home, and at first I wasn't sure how she'd relate to a mixed group of somewhat traditional church members. Yet Sally continued to come and participate each week. Soon the other group members, including two elderly women, a single mom, and two middle-aged couples with their children, became like a family to her. The relationships that Sally developed through the intergenerational experience helped her get through some very rough times and are a major reason why Sally is such a strong Christian woman today.

Another intergenerational experience occurred in a church in Chicago where I served as youth pastor. My first challenge was to mend the many wounds that developed as a result of a well-liked youth pastor being asked to leave. Since the pain of the experience was being shared by some of the parents and other adults who had been accused of running the former youth pastor off, it was obvious that an effective solution had to involve both youth and adults. After seeking input from teens, parents, and other church leaders, I put together a four-week Sunday school class for parents and their teenagers that focused on relationship building. The purpose of the class was to provide an opportunity for both generations to communicate, share, understand, trust, and accept one another unconditionally.

I can still remember the class that focused on honoring one another. A teenager who had not spoken warmly to his mother in years, with tears in his eyes, thanked her in front of the group for something special she had done many years before. Something very special happened that day, both in the lives of that family and in the hearts of the other parents and teens in the class. Once the emotional ice was broken, the Holy Spirit began to move rapidly to provide healing and restoration. Before the class was finished, I had a waiting list for the next one; and by the time the third class rolled around, I was totally convinced of the importance of intergenerational group experiences.

> *A teenager who had not spoken warmly to his mother in years, with tears in his eyes, thanked her in front of the group for something special she had done for him many years before.*

A third example of an intergenerational small-group experience happened in another church in the Chicago area. I was given an opportunity to plan an intergenerational retreat for the whole church focusing on personal and interpersonal growth. The unique feature of the retreat was that most of the intimate learning experiences occurred within the context of small intergenerational sharing groups.

Single adults were mixed together with families to provide a rich, extended family atmosphere. The small groups worked together all weekend and reported what they had learned in the large-group gatherings. The setting challenged all participants, from different age groups and stages in life, to listen, exercise patience, show sensitivity, and express themselves more creatively to one another. I can still remember one group, made up of sixteen people from ages four to eighty, enthusiastically rummaging together through stacks of old magazines searching for pictures representing what it means to grow. The scene included older people and teens helping children cut out pictures, children getting excited about finding the perfect picture, and most importantly the Body of Christ laughing and learning together. Later, when the group shared their finished product with everyone else, it was a moving experience to see how each participant related to his or her unique contribution to the growth collage.

Without belittling traditional learning programs, my experiences have convinced me that congregations need to intentionally design intergenerational experiences that more closely resemble the heterogeneous nature of God's family. This is especially important in today's society because of the many recent changes within the family and social structure.

Defining the Language

In order that I might more effectively explain the concept of intergenerational small group ministry, let me define a few important terms and concepts.

• **Small group.** Small groups in an intergenerational setting typically include five to twenty participants. Groups made up of fewer than five persons will be somewhat limited in creative interaction, whereas groups of twenty or more will be limited in their opportunities for intimacy. When planning intergenerational group experiences for a congregation or large group, divide the group into manageable smaller units.

• **Learning.** Learning is one of the key components of intergenerational small groups. For learning to take place, there must often be a change in attitude, thinking, or behavior related to the goals of the learning environment. While the term "ministry" involves a much broader scope of experiences, learning experiences are those that result in accomplishing specifically designed outcomes in the lives of the participants.

• **Family Ministry.** Family ministry usually relates primarily to ministry with the traditional family unit made up of a mother, father, and children. This differentiates from intergenerational ministry, which typically includes persons outside the nuclear family. Intergenerational groups are structured to include single adults, widows, children from families outside the church, and other individuals not connected to a traditional family. People of all ages, backgrounds, and connections can become part of intergenerational small groups.

• **Intergenerational.** For a learning experience to be truly intergenerational, it must involve at least two or more generations. Normally this would include people from two or more of the following age groups: children (birth to twelve), youth (thirteen to nineteen), young adults (twenty to thirty-five), middle adults (thirty-six to retirement), and older adults (retirement). Even within these broad divisions, there may be reasons to further subdivide based on need.

For an intergenerational event to be interactive, the focus of communication must be among the participants rather than between the leader and the participants.

• **Intentional and mission oriented.** The types of experiences discussed in this chapter are more than a few loosely structured events or experiences involving intergenerational family units. Intergenerational small-group events must be planned with specific goals and objectives in mind and must be based on the needs of the participants.

• **Interactive.** While most church worship services are intergenerational, they usually aren't interactive. Ironically, many family-life conferences and seminars, while designed to improve relationships within the family, seldom involve intergenerational interaction. For an intergenerational event to be interactive, the focus of communication must be among the participants rather than between the leader and the participants. All persons in an intergenerational group should be encouraged to communicate with someone from a different age group at least once during the meeting or event. Many times the interaction will happen spontaneously as the result of well-planned questions or activities.

> *Ironically, many family-life conferences and seminars, while designed to improve relationships within the family, seldom involve intergenerational interaction.*

Another important point that relates closely to group interaction is that group leaders should refrain from doing or saying anything that other members of the group could do, say, discover, experience, or express by themselves.

Designing Intergenerational Learning Experiences

It is difficult for the untrained eye to observe a well-planned intergenerational experience and recognize that it is based upon a distinctive structure built on several basic components.

Scott Miles, an experienced designer of active family-learning programs has identified five distinctive components of intergenerational learning events: *activity, simplicity, informality, celebration,* and *involvement.* [1]

• **Activity.** A vital element of intergenerational learning is activity. Purposeful activity provides a way for persons of all ages to work and play together. Children, teenagers, and adults alike will build stronger insights from practical, hands-on learning experiences. Groups that include children definitely should include a variety of active-learning experiences.

An activity serves as a catalyst for interpersonal communication and interaction among persons of various age groups. An activity such as cutting out pictures from magazines or a scavenger hunt will help both young and old to build bridges of communication and grow spiritually. A well-chosen activity gives participants of all ages a common frame of reference for interacting with a particular topic or issue.

Children, teenagers, and adults alike will build stronger insights from practical, hands-on learning experiences.

• **Simplicity.** Jesus was a master at making complicated topics simple for the benefit of his hearers. In Matthew 6:25-27, Jesus illustrated God's care for people by using a simple illustration of how God cares for the birds. It's ironic that, although Jesus was perfect in wisdom and knowledge, he was able to communicate simply and clearly to persons of all ages without sacrificing depth.

Intergenerational learning experiences must follow the principle of simplicity in order to insure that all participants will grasp the main idea of the lesson. Lessons and activities should be meaningful to all age levels represented in the small group. Scott Miles suggests that we "plan activities that even the youngest family members are able to participate in with help from older family members." [2]

An older adult may learn a simple Bible principle more by helping a younger child or teenager learn it than by reflecting upon it in a traditional setting with peers.

An older adult may learn a simple Bible principle more by helping a younger child or teenager learn it than by reflecting upon it in a traditional setting with peers.

• **Informality.** If you think back to some of the most significant learning experiences you've had with a family member, one of the distinctive elements will probably be informality. Some of the most special times in my own family have come from shooting the breeze, paddling in a canoe, shivering together in a tent, jogging, riding in the car, and doing chores together.

One of the keys for successful intergenerational groups is to know how to maintain an appropriate level of informality. A relaxed physical environment and casual dress will help set an informal tone. An informal home environment will obviously be much more comfortable and intimate than a church classroom. Informality, however, is in no way related to the absence of planning or structure. Every aspect of the intergenerational group experience, including the informal atmosphere, must be carefully planned, especially when children are involved as participants. This is one of the primary differences between a traditional small-group meeting and one that includes several age groups. The attention span of a child is obviously different from that of an adult, and planned activities are the best way to keep kids tied into the group experience.

• **Celebration.** One of the foremost characteristics of an intergenerational group experience is having fun together. The highlight of most successful experiences in this context is celebration. Celebration means the group's ability to enjoy periodic experiences of laughing and having fun together. Just as a sign of a healthy family is its ability to laugh together, one of the elements of a healthy small group is its ability to have fun together.

Just as a sign of a healthy family is its ability to laugh together, one of the elements of a healthy small group is its ability to have fun together.

The diverse makeup of intergenerational groups demands that members exercise both flexibility and restraint in their use of humor and joking, however. It is important to refrain from focusing on more vulnerable group members in the form of sarcasm or insensitivity.

• **Involvement.** One of the more obvious elements of an intergenerational small-group experience is involvement of every member of the group in the activities. Yet this is also one of the most difficult elements to deal with. The tendency of many intergenerational groups is for one particular age group to dominate. This often leads to people within the group feeling marginalized and bored.

Group leaders need to carefully plan each activity to ensure that even the youngest child or the most elderly adult can take part at some level. Leaders must be careful not to build all of the learning events around dialogue and discussion that alienates the more "hands-on" learners. A good way to ensure the involvement at each age level is to plan a variety of activities, including drama, role-play, skits, object lessons, and various forms of artistic expression.

Designing a Small-Group Intergenerational Event

To effectively plan a small-group intergenerational event, a group leader should take the following steps:

• **Step One: Choose a planning team.**

The first step in designing an intergenerational small-group ministry or event is to establish a multigenerational team to help plan and implement it. Building a broad base of support from the beginning will help ensure success. Encouraging input from persons of all ages in the planning stage will also help provide a more balanced approach. Each step should be taken as a team, with certain aspects of each step delegated to a person within the team gifted in a particular area. While it may not be appropriate to have young children present at all the team planning meetings, their input may be helpful.

• **Step Two: Establish the learning needs of the group.**

Evaluating the learning needs of an intergenerational group is typically more complex than that of a single-age group. The reasons are quite obvious. For example, it would be unwise to pick a topic such as "sanctification" for an intergenerational study. Most children and some teenagers will have difficulty understanding a topic stated in these terms. It would be much better to state it in terms such as "growing to be more like Jesus." Children, youth, and adults can all identify a topic stated this way.

• **Step Three: Identify goals and objectives.**

Once the learning needs of the group have been identified, it's important to determine the goals. Goals should always be stated in terms of what the learner will *know, be,* or *do.* By focusing on what the participants will learn rather than on what the teacher will teach, a lesson will be much more learner-centered and definitely more fruitful for an intergenerational group.

For example, if a learning need is to "grow to be more like Jesus," a possible goal might be "for each person to identify what he or she must do to grow to be more like Jesus." A goal stated in this way focuses on *knowing* and *doing* and will actually help participants become motivated "to grow to be more like Jesus."

By focusing on what the participants will learn rather than on what the teacher will teach, a lesson will be much more learner-centered and definitely more fruitful for an intergenerational group.

While each lesson needs only one major goal, a goal may have three objectives. An objective provides the steps the learner will take in order to accomplish the goal. The objectives may also focus on *knowing, being,* or *doing.* If the goal was "that each person desire to grow to be more like Jesus," three objectives might be similar to these:

1. Participants identify areas in their lives where they need to improve;

2. Participants understand reasons why they need to grow more like Jesus;

3. Participants identify attributes of Jesus they'd like to incorporate into their own lives.

The more clearly the objectives are stated, the easier it will be to pick appropriate Scriptures and design helpful activities.

• Step Four: Design the best learning environment.

Once clear goals and objectives have been stated, the next task is to choose the best learning environment to accomplish them. The type of learning context should be directly related to the goals that have been identified. For example, if the goal is related to helping participants "learn to serve others," the best environment might be one provided by a group service project. If the goal is to "learn respect for others," spending an afternoon visiting residents in a nursing home might create an effective learning environment. Employing a wide variety of learning environments will help participants have memorable, life-changing experiences.

Settings outside the confines of a church building will typically provide the most fruitful environment for intergenerational learning. Homes, camps, retreat centers, and mission locations provide ideal environments for informal learning. Some of the best intergenerational group experiences involve a regular weekly meeting in a home with a longer, more creative experience monthly, such as a service project, celebration experience, or family meal.

• **Step Five: Zero in on Scripture.**

Scripture should provide the foundation for learning that occurs in an intergenerational group. However, care needs to be taken when identifying ways to incorporate Scripture into activities. Team members who are charged with planning a lesson should keep the group's youngest person in mind when deciding how the Scriptures will be applied.

Team members who are charged with planning a lesson should keep the group's youngest person in mind when deciding how the Scriptures will be applied.

The *keep-it-simple* concept is particularly relevant to an intergenerational setting. One way of doing this is by a passage's "big idea." The big idea of the passage needs to be stated in a way that the youngest member of the group can relate to. This statement then becomes the focal point of the learning experience. Examples of big ideas are the following:

- Mark 4:21-23—If we really love Jesus we will show him to others.
- Matthew 13:31-32—God can make big things out of small things.
- Ruth 1:16-17—Real friendship means commitment.
- Psalm 145:18—God's ears are open to those who are pure.

When working with groups of combined ages and understanding, it is important to keep the content simple without being unnecessarily simplistic. Stories, illustrations, parables, and simple analogies often have the broadest application in an intergenerational context.

• **Step Six: Design learning activities.**

Real learning takes place in a person's life only when attitudes, thinking, perceptions, or actions change. Every method and activity in an intergenerational event must be planned with such an intentional learning goal in mind.

The learning activity itself, however, should never become the primary focus; rather, it's important to remain focused on the goals and objectives established for each lesson.

It's often helpful to divide a group learning event into three components and create a lesson accordingly:

1. Priming the pump for learning

• Role play, pantomime, drama, skit, story telling, or video

• Music

• Games, object lessons, show and tell, treasure hunt

• Reporting on current events

• Brainstorming, word association, sharing personal history

2. Exploring the big idea

• Acting out the Bible story, pantomime, expressive storytelling

• Constructing a time line with significant events in a story

• Graphing the ups and downs of a character's life

• Mock interviews with a biblical character

• Mapping out a biblical character's journey

3. Applying the big idea

• Role-play, practicing skills, acting out desired behaviors

• Problem solving related to life situation, brainstorming

• Projects, group plans, group covenants

• Writing, drawing, singing—expressing response in various artistic form

• Prayer: singing, written, conversational, partners, acted out to God

• Planning, contracting, scheduling with accountability

Developing an Intergenerational Small-Group Ministry

• Start by developing an intergenerational planning team. Prayerfully choose a group of creative people with representatives from each age category. Give this group as much freedom as possible in carrying out the other steps. Communicate your plans with the church board and other appropriate leadership.

• Do some research. Investigate what other creative churches are doing with intergenerational groups. Collect curriculum samples and books that relate to intergenerational events and lessons.

Two excellent curriculum resources for intergenerational groups are *Family Sunday School Specials* by Tim Smith, available from Group Publishing, and a series entitled *Families Learning Together* by Karyn Henley, available through Standard Publishing.

• Provide opportunities for congregational discussion about the benefits of an intergenerational small-group ministry. This is an important step in selling the vision to others and may provide some helpful input and new ideas.

• Examine the overall ministry of the congregation, and identify current programs where intergenerational small groups will work best. Will they fit in the Sunday school program? midweek program? vacation Bible school? children's ministry? or a traditional small-group program?

• Start small, possibly with only one intergenerational group. Develop it as a pilot program, and allow various opportunities for feedback and assessment.

• Begin by setting specific goals that you want to accomplish in an intergenerational ministry. Then plan the details in relation to your goals. Map out details, including such things as curriculum, leadership, service opportunities, location and time of meeting, participants, and publicity.

• Provide leadership training for those who will be facilitating the group. Training should include standard small-group dynamics as well as elements that are unique to intergenerational groups.

• Meet regularly with the leadership team to encourage the completion of the assigned tasks and to evaluate progress of the ministry.

Endnotes

1. M. Scott Miles, *Families Growing Together,* Victor Books, 1990, 31-37.

2. Miles, *Families Growing Together,* 33.

CHAPTER 4

Small-Group Strategies to Reach Generation X

PAUL A. KAAK

*Paul Kaak is pastor of global extension at New Song Church
and a staff member with the Leadership Institute, both based
in southern California. A Gen Xer himself, Paul has been
serving Generation X as a pastor and small-group leader for
several years.*

More Than a Program

The people who make up the demographic segment of our society known as "Generation X," (myself included) are often referred to as "gripers" and "whiners." This really shouldn't be surprising because, in many respects, Gen Xers believe they received the raw end of the socioeconomic deal. Our generational predecessors, "the Boomers," looked as if they had everything going for them. As time went on, however, the Boomer "get-it-while-you-can" experiment failed, and the result was a generation feeling as though they'd been left to sweep up a familial, economic, and spiritual trash heap.

Many Gen Xers have turned away from the institutional church, including traditional approaches to small-group ministry that they feel are too inauthentic and programmatic.

While these criticisms are undoubtedly overstated, one of the unfortunate byproducts is that many Gen Xers have turned away from the institutional church, including traditional approaches to small-group ministry that they feel are inauthentic and too programmatic.

Gen Xer theologian Tom Beaudoin says, "Generation X approaches religion with a lived theology that is very suspicious of institutions. Indeed, Xers have a heavily ingrained (one could say "institutional") suspicion or skepticism (even cynicism) in general. This skepticism surfaces most acutely in regard to those who purport to be looking out for the generation's good. As the self-appointed guardians of Xers'—and all—souls, religious institutions are therefore frequent objects of Gen X criticism." [1]

Both Christian and non-Christian Xers have a prophetic word for the church and, specifically, a word about how small-group ministries can remain relevant and successfully make a transition into the twenty-first century.

However, before you tune out their laments, take time to listen to the combined voice of Generation X! They are definitely saying something worth hearing. Both Christian and non-Christian Xers have a prophetic word for the church and, specifically, a word about how small-group ministries can remain relevant and successfully make a transition into the twenty-first century.

Listen first to the voice of the non-Christian Gen Xers. Here are a few criticisms they typically have of the church:

- Its people (especially its leaders) are *hypocrites*.
- Its teachings are *irrelevant* to the issues of the real world.
- Its attitude is *intolerant* and *unaccepting* of people who are "different" from its typical membership.
- Its spirituality is *dry* and *boring*.

Many Christian Gen Xers, on the other hand, grew up in the church and while they know its language, they aren't hearing the voice of the Good Shepherd so clearly. Hear what they are saying about the church:

- Its people (especially its leaders) are *inauthentic*.
- Its teachings are *impractical*, perhaps relevant, but useless.
- Its attitude is *shaming*.
- Its spirituality is *all intellect* and *no experience*.

Whether or not church leaders believe these criticisms are true, at the very least, they are perceptions that are keeping most non-Christian Gen Xers from giving the church a chance. In addition, they are motivating many Christian Gen Xers to bail out.

The motivation behind this chapter is not so much to address these perceptions as it is to answer the question of whether or not a small-group ministry can provide a sense of authentic Christianity for Gen Xers.

Let me abruptly answer that question by saying, "No! A small-group ministry can't address the needs of Gen Xers, at least not in the traditional sense of the small-group experience."

Recently a friend of mine, who is also a Gen X pastor, said, "In my experience, traditional small groups destroy community."

I knew exactly what he meant. I thought to myself, "I've been in those groups. But what's even worse, I've

> *Recently, a friend of mine, who is also a Gen X pastor, said, "In my experience, traditional small groups destroy community." I knew exactly what he meant. I thought to myself, "I've been in those groups. But what's even worse, I've led those groups."*

led those groups." I remember being so proud of myself as a small-group leader when I could squeeze a one-and-a-half-hour lesson from two verses in the Bible. Interaction? No time! Worship? Hardly! Intercession? Only if we had to. Intimacy? Doubtful! Jesus? Well...

Like me, my wife has been in the church all her life. After growing up in a broken home, as a young adult she began searching for a church that would provide a sense of healing and community. What she discovered, however, like many in our generation, is that most churches today provide little sense of authentic community. What's more, she doubted that this was what Jesus intended for the church as he modeled community with his small group of disciples.

My wife was ready to give up on the church altogether, but she decided to give it one last chance. Together we joined a small group of twelve people and quickly discovered that their approach to the small-group experience was different than we'd ever experienced. People shared from the depths of their joy and pain; people shared their stories about how God's word had changed their lives; together we all worshipped God in simple yet profound ways; we moved out of our comfort zones and touched the lives of lost and hurting people. As all this happened, my wife was able to believe in church again. This small group of imperfect yet authentic people became the church she'd always dreamed of.

> *As all this happened, my wife was able to believe in church again. This small group of imperfect yet authentic people became the church she'd always dreamed of.*

According to Tom Beaudoin, "A new sort of Gen X liberation theology is emerging, but it is not primarily about the poor...Instead, it begins with the liberation of Jesus from the clutches of the church. Jesus himself needs to be liberated so that Xers can experience the power of his words and deeds, the blessing of his bodily and spiritual presence." [2]

Small groups that liberate the power of Christ from the clutches of the traditional church can provide a sense of authentic community for

> *Small groups that liberate the power of Christ from the clutches of the traditional church can provide a sense of authentic community for Gen Xers and bring them back into the church.*

Gen Xers and bring them back into the church. So the answer to the question of whether a small-group ministry can provide a sense of authentic Christianity for Gen Xers is "Yes, if it's both real and truly life changing!"

Characteristics of Generation X

If you don't already know, you should be aware that talking about "Generation X" is passé—especially among Generation Xers. As one who has been providing ministry to my generation long before they were being profiled, two things have become abundantly clear:

1. Gen Xers don't like to be labeled or profiled; and

2. Gen Xers represent more of a shift in the dominant Western worldview than merely a statistical category.

So if Generation X is predominately comprised of a group of "gripers" and "whiners" and since they don't like to be profiled, why give them any attention at all?

Let me answer that question by suggesting three significant reasons why their issues need to be more than just interesting topics for trend watchers:

1. Just as a missionary would study the culture and values of a country in which he or she was going to minister, church leaders today must seek to understand Gen Xers if they're going to reach them for Christ;

2. Gen X is comprised of those people who will be the next generation to take over and lead the church; and

3. Gen Xers can make significant contributions when it comes to understanding authentic small-group experiences.

Roughly, those born between 1965 and 1985 comprise what is known as Generation X. In a sense, this generation serves history as a transitional generation, bridging the gap from modernism to postmodernism.

Roughly, those born between 1965 and 1985 comprise what is known as Generation X. In a sense, this generation serves history as a transitional generation, bridging the gap from modernism to postmodernism.

Postmodern simply means, "that which comes after the modern." If postmodernism is characterized by the microprocessor and the Web, Gen X is characterized as a group of people whose parents both worked outside the home to provide a "better life"—and ended up divorced. It's characterized by its earliest memory of a president as one who resigned in disgrace and by the sexual revolution degenerating into fear that free sex meant early death. It's characterized by a fear of economic instability upon reaching the age of retirement.

This transitional generation has significant implications for the church. For the church to be relevant to Generation X, while at the same time being true to the biblical challenge to spread the Gospel, it must provide opportunities for authentic community and Christian growth.

Wouldn't it be great if the church, soon to be led by Gen X and their younger siblings, the Millenials, would bring the good news of our Lord into a global culture that is searching for moral and spiritual bearings!

Creating Community for the X Gen

One of the byproducts of being part of this transitional generation is the longing for a sense of authentic community. In his book *Community and Social Change in America*, author Thomas Bender begins to define the Gen X understanding of community. Bender says, "[I]t is clear from the many layers of emotional meaning attached to the word *community* that the concept means more than a place of local activity. There is an expectation of a special quality of human relationship in a community, and it is this experiential dimension that is crucial to its definition. Community, then, can be defined better as an experience than as a place. As simply as possible, community is where community happens." [3]

Psychologically, an Xer will define community as a group where he or she belongs, is

> **P**sychologically, *an Xer will define community as a group where he or she belongs, is accepted, and finds hope for both the present and future.*

accepted, and finds hope for both the present and future. *Spiritually*, the same person might say that community is where he or she experiences God and grapples with how to live alongside God and others. For the Xer, such a *community* essentially becomes *church* when it's safe, fun, meaningful, interactive, and healing.

> *The difficulty in speaking about models to Gen Xers is that it's very "postmodern" to reject anyone who comes up with "the model" for something...Some Gen Xers, a bit tongue in cheek perhaps, speak of postmodelism right alongside the concept of postmodernism.*

There are those who claim to have the "perfect model" for Gen X small groups. The difficulty in speaking about models to Gen Xers is that it's very "postmodern" to reject anyone who comes up with "the model" for something. Gen Xers see it as arrogant when a leader says, "This is it!" Some Gen Xers, a bit tongue in cheek perhaps, speak of *postmodelism* right alongside the concept of *postmodernism*. Having said that, however, many Gen Xers are very passionate about the kind of community that can happen in a small-group setting.

A Cell-Group Approach for Generation X

There are several approaches to small-group ministries that have been successful for Generation X. In many ways the word "cell" describes the nature of an authentic group much better than any other word. Cell groups are, in a very real sense, a microcosm of the church and serve as much more than a church program.

> *The "cell" is an exciting way to visualize Christian community. A cell is living, growing, moving, and life-giving. When we speak of cell groups, we aren't talking about lifeless, static, or fossilized assemblages.*

Give consideration for a moment to the true meaning of a "cell." Biological studies suggest that "the cell is the smallest unit of biological activity that displays the special attributes by which we characterize life." [4] The "cell" is an exciting way to visualize Christian community. A cell is living, growing, moving, and life-giving. When we speak of cell groups, we aren't talking about lifeless, static, or fossilized assemblages. Christian community within a cell group, the kind that connects with Gen Xers, has energy and purpose, but it is flexible enough to meet the needs of people in an ever-changing world.

If the objective of cell groups is merely getting people into groups, the primary purpose of a cell-group ministry has been seriously misunderstood. Cell groups are meant for disciple making, not merely assimilation. The challenge of Jesus' great commission (Matthew 28:18-20) has taught us the importance of assimilating people into our churches. But bringing new people into the church merely to assimilate them into programs neglects the true purpose of the church. Cell-group ministries that make a difference are those that help people deepen their intimacy with one another, and with God.

> *If the objective of cell groups is merely that of getting people into groups, the primary purpose of a cell-group ministry has been seriously misunderstood. Cell groups are meant for disciple making, not merely assimilation.*

There are many ways to discuss the mission of the local church community. Most church leaders would agree, however, that the church has three primary purposes: an upward purpose to worship God; an inward purpose of fellowship and equipping people for ministry; and finally, an outward purpose for making disciples of all nations.

As a microcosm of the church, an authentic cell group is designed to live out these purposes in the simplicity of a community of five to twelve people. In order to be successful, cell groups must seek out an appropriate balance of all three. Here are several principles that need to be included in each cell-group meeting:

• A reconnecting activity

This is a specific time in the group when leaders challenge individuals to interact with each other. This may include an icebreaker, a simple game, a relevant question for discussion, a chance to share personal updates, or a snack to share. *Fun Friend-Making Activities for Adult Groups,* available from Group Publishing, offers some excellent ideas for these activities.

• A time of worship

Worship in the cell-group setting is an opportunity for participants to acknowledge Christ as the reason they come together in the first place. Through various forms of musical and nonmusical worship, individuals should be given opportunities to center their hearts on the Lord and invite the Holy Spirit to be present.

• Focus on God's Word

Effective cell groups should allow God's Word to set the stage for their lives and relationships. This is typically accomplished in the form of a study or pointed discussion, though not as lengthy as a traditional Bible study.

• Affirmation and encouragement

A successful cell group needs to allow time for members to encourage one another. This can be done through shared stories, prayer, or personal affirmations. It's also a time when tears and hugs are shared.

• Focus on prayer and service

Important to each meeting are the moments spent intentionally praying for needs that go beyond those of the group. It's also important for participants to take time to discuss plans for mission and service beyond the group itself. This can be anything from a one-evening local service opportunity to a short-term mission project.

Making Room for the Holy Spirit

The agenda for a specific cell-group meeting needs to be simple and flexible enough to allow opportunities for the Holy Spirit to work.

A friend of mine recently worked very hard to develop the necessary skills to lead a cell group. He was finally ready to lead his first meeting. As the meeting began, Lance took out his thirteen pages of handwritten notes and presented a lesson. The content was biblically solid and quite interesting. His preparation was obviously very thorough. As

I sat through the meeting, however, I noticed that it seemed to lack a sense of power and intimacy. It lacked the sense of God's presence. I finally discovered why. The meeting was packed so full of content and structure that it lacked the flexibility to respond to the needs of the participants. There was no room for the Holy Spirit to work.

A balanced but flexible agenda is key for effective cell groups. Space needs to be provided in every meeting for people to share and for the Holy Spirit to work. When flexibility is intentionally woven into each meeting, what might otherwise be just another meeting has the potential to become a powerful group experience.

A balanced but flexible agenda is key for effective cell groups. Space needs to be provided in every meeting for people to share and for the Holy Spirit to work. When flexibility is intentionally woven into each meeting, what might otherwise be just another meeting has the potential to become a powerful group experience.

Internal and External Components

Our church made the initial mistake of calling our groups "care groups." A problem quickly surfaced as participants wrestled with understanding the primary purpose of the groups. Tension emerged between participants who sensed the primary mission as taking care of the needs of one another and those who sensed the purpose as reaching out into the local community. "We aren't about serving others," some participants would brood. "We are a care group, caring for each other!"

Even today, though we've changed the name of our cell groups, many participants haven't been able to break from believing that cell groups are exclusively about serving one another rather than reaching out to those beyond the group.

To be totally authentic, groups need to recognize that they need both internal and external components. Effective cell groups are on a mission into the world, not just a mission to

To be totally authentic, groups need to recognize that they need both internal and external components. Effective cell groups are on a mission into the world, not just a mission to care for themselves.

care for themselves. To help participants understand this concept, I often use an illustration that compares groups to either a battleship or a cruise ship.

On a Cruise Ship:	On a Battleship:
People expect to be served.	People expect to serve.
On a Cruise Ship: The staff takes care of the passengers.	**On a Battleship:** Those on board take care of one another.
On a Cruise Ship: Gratification comes from the comfort and beautiful scenery.	**On a Battleship:** Gratification comes from participating in the mission.
On a Cruise Ship: Relationships are superficial.	**On a Battleship:** Relationships are close-knit and meaningful.
On a Cruise Ship: Not much is expected of the passengers.	**On a Battleship:** Every person has an assignment and participates in the mission.
On a Cruise Ship: The thrill comes from the food and service.	**On a Battleship:** The thrill comes from accomplishing the mission.

The comparison between the two ships illustrates the importance of cell groups to maintain a balance between internal and external components. Authentic cell groups should reach out into the world and share the urgency of their mission with others.

The following excerpt from *Missional Church* summarizes this point well: "The experience of Christian togetherness is not simply for the benefit of those who choose to participate in Christian community. A community of love rooted in the redemptive reign of God can never be an in-house enterprise, for such love is contagious and overflowing." [5]

Authenticity Within Cell Groups

I've been using the word "authentic" to talk about what Gen Xers expect from their relationships, whether in a small-group setting or the church at large. For cell-group experiences to be truly authentic and appeal to Gen Xers, they must include several vital components. A group that fails to include any of these components will open itself to claims of being inauthentic and will thus have limited effect in reaching Gen Xers.

• Relationships valued as much as biblical teaching

Even as I put this component on paper, I squirm in my seat. Personally, I place very high value of the Word of God, accurate biblical interpretation, and propositional truth. To say that my generation is more concerned with relationships than biblical teaching sounds almost heretical. It's simply a statement of fact that Gen Xers would rather be loved than lectured to.

While this perceived pendulum swing from objective truth to subjective relationships frightens some church leaders, they should remember that Jesus himself put a high value on authentic relationships and community. Jesus stated, "This is my command: Love each other" (John 15:17).

> *It is simply a statement of fact that Gen Xers would rather be loved than lectured to.*

The Apostle Paul also understood the importance of authentic relationships; he wrote, "From him the whole body, joined and held together by every supporting ligament, grows and builds itself up in love, as each part does its work" (Ephesians 4:16).

• Learning through stories and active experiences

Since they were children, Gen Xers have been immersed in stories, whether they are about a man named Brady, a group of teenagers and

Stories of all kinds, both good and bad, have helped form the moral conscience of Generation X. The positive consequence is that they make a receptive audience for storytelling. Since stories are the milieu of the Bible, Gen X cell-group leaders are presented with a unique opportunity for presenting God's Word.

their happy days at Arnold's Diner, a group known as "Friends" or the story of Luke, Han, and Leia. Stories of all kinds, both good and bad, have helped form the moral conscience of Generation X. The positive consequence is that they make a receptive audience for storytelling. Since stories are the milieu of the Bible, Gen X cell-group leaders are presented with a unique opportunity for presenting God's Word.

Biblical stories only make sense for them, however, when they are presented in the context of personal experience. Gen Xers don't learn well from bullet-point presentations. They learn the truths of Scripture most effectively when they are presented in the context of real experiences. Many of the Old Testament wisdom writers would undoubtedly agree. For them, the wisdom of the proverbs was accumulated through experiences of observing people and nature.

Gen Xers don't learn well from bullet-point presentations. They learn the truths of Scripture most effectively when they are presented in the context of real experiences.

Gen Xers are also open to learning through active experiences. For example, a cell group might grow a plant and discuss how it resembles God's providing nourishment for people to grow and mature. A group might watch a video together and discuss how it relates to their faith. A group might eat a meal together and discuss the issue of spiritual nourishment. Or a group might pray for people in other countries using a map of the world or photos from National Geographic. Experiential learning possibilities are endless.

A cell group might grow a plant and discuss how it resembles God's providing nourishment for people to grow and mature.

A group might watch a video together and discuss how it relates to their faith.

A group might eat a meal together and discuss the issue of spiritual nourishment.

A group might pray for people in other countries using a map of the world or photos from National Geographic.

Service projects also serve as very effective active-learning experiences for Gen X cell groups. For example, group members might provide a free car wash and later discuss the concept of Christian service. They might throw a party for international students and discuss God's love for all people. They might sponsor a blood drive and discuss how Christ shed his blood for the forgiveness of sin. They might clean up the beach and discuss the importance of caring for God's creation. They might visit a nursing home and discuss the importance of caring for those who are sick and lonely. The sky, of course, is the limit!

Rather than criticizing Gen X's need to process biblical truths through active-learning experiences, church leaders should praise the Gen X desire to see their faith lived out in real life.

Pastors and leaders who intentionally seek to build groups for Gen X need to provide opportunities for them to tie biblical truth to stories and active experiences. As Tom Beaudoin notes in his book *Virtual Faith*, "Xers generally find the religious in personal experience...In this turn to experience, there is a constant yearning, both implicit and explicit, for the almost mystical encounter of the human and divine. This turn to experience also manifests in a new interest in communities of faith, as well as in faith lived in the everyday experience of the world." [6]

• **Shared leadership**

Group leadership is an important issue for Gen Xers. They are definitely suspicious of leaders whose authority is based on titles, education, or position. Rather than providing a leadership monopoly for one or two people, effective Gen X cell groups need to provide opportunities for all participants to lead and develop leadership skills. Discerning leaders will accomplish this by making room for participants to share their talents and gifts as part of the group process. The goal is twofold: (1) to strengthen the confidence of participants and

(2) to prepare others for future leadership roles in cell groups and other positions within the church.

When intentional leadership opportunities are provided within a group, people who didn't previously picture themselves in positions of leadership will begin to develop the confidence to do so. Besides, the continued success of a small-group ministry depends upon the effectiveness of leadership development. One of the goals of a cell group is to give birth to new groups. Without new leaders, however, the future of a cell-group ministry is dubious at best. So in one sense, a primary purpose of cell groups is to prepare people for future group leadership.

One of the goals of a cell group is to give birth to new groups. Without new leaders, however, the future of a cell-group ministry is dubious at best. So in one sense, a primary purpose of cell groups is to prepare people for future group leadership.

Henri Nouwen provides meaningful insight into the kind of leadership that is most effective in reaching Gen X: "[T]rue ministry must be mutual. When the members of a community of faith cannot truly know and love their shepherd, shepherding quickly becomes a subtle way of exercising power over others and begins to show authoritarian and dictatorial traits…The leadership about which Jesus speaks is of a radically different kind from the leadership offered by the world. It is servant leadership…in which the leader is a vulnerable servant who needs the people as much as they need him or her." [7]

Many Gen X cell groups have failed simply because leaders took total control rather than allowing opportunities for participants to use and develop their leadership skills.

Many Gen X cell groups have failed simply because leaders took total control rather than allowing opportunities for participants to use and develop their leadership skills.

Whenever I provide training for cell-group leaders, I try to model a good facilitator as one who talks the least and demonstrate how a group leader needs to become, first and foremost, a participating member of the group.

• **Tolerance of people in various stages of life**

Cell groups are intended to include anyone who is interested in seriously pursuing a relationship with Jesus Christ. They aren't exclusively for spiritual seekers or the spiritually mature. Healthy cell groups will typically contain a variety of participants all at different places along the Christian journey.

A healthy cell-group ministry should also seek to include participants with a variety of Christian backgrounds and traditions. The most powerful group experiences I have been involved with were those that included people from different denominational and religious backgrounds.

One of the highest values for Gen Xers is that of tolerance. In many Christian circles, the word "tolerance" takes on a negative connotation and implies an acceptance and infiltration of non-Christian values; from a Gen X point of view, however, it implies respect for others. For a cell group to be authentic, participants must be respected for who they are and at the same time be challenged to grow in Christian faith. Groups that make an impact on the lives of Gen Xers will be inclusive, not exclusive.

> *One of the highest values for Gen Xers is that of tolerance. In many Christian circles the word "tolerance" takes on a negative connotation and implies an acceptance and infiltration of non-Christian values; from a Gen X point of view, however, it implies respect for others.*

• Loyalty to Jesus, not an institution

Good cell groups are not about building an organization, whether it is a church or a parachurch group. A primary function of cell groups is to invite others into a deeper love relationship with Christ. If Gen Xers sense that groups are focused more on denominational loyalties and hierarchical organizations than on building authentic relationships, they will typically have no part!

• A week-long commitment to Christ

Most Gen Xers who were raised in the church have a deep longing for an authentic relationship with Christ, and yet few have any memorable models of it. As I grew up in church, I felt as though being a Christian had more to do with a checklist of things to do than

Since authenticity is such a high value for Gen Xers, they have a very tuned-in "bogus spirituality detector." They don't understand how people can show up at church on Sunday and then move into their week with no apparent connection with the people or ideas they were exposed to."

developing intimate relationships with Christ and other Christians.

Since authenticity is such a high value for Gen Xers, they have a very tuned-in "bogus spirituality detector." They don't understand how people can show up at church on Sunday and then move into their week with no apparent connection with the people or ideas they were exposed to. Gen Xers will rarely participate in churches or groups that they sense are filled with Sunday-only Christians. They aren't expecting perfection and are quick to acknowledge their own shortcomings. Their desire, however, is to belong to a group or church whose members demonstrate an ongoing commitment to Christ.

Ten Strategies for Creating Effective Gen X Groups

Here are a few strategies that will help create effective cell-group experiences for Generation X.

1. Start from the bottom up rather than the top down.

The traditional way to cast a vision for a new program or ministry is for the senior pastor to do it. However, since Gen Xers are often skeptical of leadership and typically mistrust hierarchical structures, instituting a new cell-group ministry will be more successful if it takes the form of a grass-roots movement. The best way to start a cell-group ministry is to start as Jesus did—by intentionally gathering a few people together rather than bringing a program down from the mountaintop and imposing it on the people.

2. Provide adequate support, training, and resources for leaders.

One of our early mistakes with cell groups was to identify, train, and motivate leaders and then turn them loose without any plans to provide them ongoing support.

A vital part of an effective cell-group ministry is to provide leaders with support and encouragement. Whether the title is coach, mentor, or consultant, the object is to provide group leaders with a support person. Training resources are vital, but it's a leader's knowledge that someone is available for emotional support and encouragement that makes the difference between a group that's successful and one that isn't.

> *Training resources are vital, but it's a leader's knowledge that someone is available for emotional support and encouragement that makes the difference between a group that's successful and one that isn't.*

3. Supplement ongoing groups with short-term special interest groups.

Many individuals have specific needs that can't always be dealt with adequately in a regular cell-group setting. These needs include such things as support and recovery from abuse, divorce, and illness. Any effective cell-group ministry should include specific short-term groups to address special ministry needs of the congregation. The content of these groups can range anywhere from a twelve-step recovery program to a weekend prayer retreat. Supplementing ongoing cell groups with short-term special interest groups will add depth to any small-group ministry.

4. Give groups permission to minister to the needs of people.

The more I read the New Testament, the more I'm convinced that it wasn't just religious professionals—educated, ordained, or appointed—who administered the sacraments and officiated at baptism. A very powerful way to show trust and confidence in group leaders is to train them to be involved in areas of ministry traditionally carried out by professional ministers.

At New Song Church, the entire congregation celebrates baptisms while the small-group

> *At New Song Church, the entire congregation celebrates baptisms while the small-group leaders take an active role. A pastor on staff serves as host and provides support for the baptisms, but it's actually the small-group leaders who do the baptizing.*

leaders take an active role. A pastor on staff serves as host and provides support for the baptisms, but it's actually the small-group leaders who do the baptizing. Utilizing group leaders in this way makes sense because they are the ones who typically provide guidance to new Christians. It's an awesome experience for group leaders to baptize newly committed Christians who belong to their groups.

Ministry privileges such as this, however, need to have a high degree of accountability attached. If baptisms are the regular responsibility of small-group leaders, an effective reporting system should be put in place for purposes of accountability and communication. Through a system of reporting, connecting with a coach or mentor, and ongoing leadership training, group leaders can become ministry partners with trained pastoral staff. This combination of trust and accountability will result in some very powerful group experiences.

5. Let new facilitators gather their own groups; encourage them to invite both Christians and non-Christians alike.

Gen X groups will be more successful, especially in the beginning, if they aren't *put together* by the staff. Assigning participants to a group can cause problems for two reasons: (1) The group may not feel as though there is any built-in affinity ("somebody *from way up there* randomly determined that we should be together"), and (2) the facilitator is less likely to take ownership of the group.

The most effective approach is to have each group leader put his or her own group together and rely on the staff primarily as a resource. This strategy will definitely promote a grass-roots approach to small-group ministry and will do much for building trust.

As new leaders look to their own network of acquaintances as potential members, there will undoubtedly be a mixture of both Christians and non-Christians. Inviting non-Christians to be part of a cell group should definitely be encouraged if for no other reason

Inviting non-Christians to be part of a cell group should definitely be encouraged if for no other reason than purposes of evangelism. Also, when a group's membership is made up of a combination of both, the group will typically move to a place of spiritual depth much more quickly than a predominately one-sided group.

than purposes of evangelism. Also, when a group's membership is a combination of both, the group will typically move to a place of spiritual depth much more quickly than a predominately one-sided group. Leaders should also be encouraged to invite people into their groups who are loners and may not fit the profile of a typical group participant.

6. Identify facilitators who have a balanced leadership approach.

It's quite easy to identify a gifted teacher and immediately plug that person into a cell-group leadership role. Good teachers have certain gifts that lend themselves well to the small-group experience, but these potential leaders must have other gifts as well. As I suggested earlier, cell groups need to be balanced, and teachers (especially young enthusiastic ones as I once was) often believe they have a great deal to say that everyone needs to hear, and perhaps they do. However, effective and balanced group leaders need to have the same understanding of their fellow Christians as did Paul when he said, "I myself am convinced, my brothers, that you yourselves are full of goodness, complete in knowledge and competent to instruct one another" (Romans 15:14).

7. Challenge groups to retain an outward focus.

Groups who maintain an outward focus on witness, service, and mission often move into a zone that is uncomfortable and risky. So it's understandable why some groups avoid being focused on anything but the issues of their own members. For a group to be successful over a period of time, however, mission and service must be of primary concern. Providing groups with opportunities for service and mission, while time consuming, is well worth the effort. When a group catches Jesus' vision for servanthood, the experience is not only powerful but contagious as well.

In addition, outreach provides an effective tool for both evangelism and adding new members to cell groups. As groups move out, people

Groups that add new members through evangelistic efforts will experience a sense of accomplishment in ways not experienced by those who grow only by adding members from the church roster.

will likely start coming in. Groups that add new members through evangelistic efforts will experience a sense of accomplishment in ways not experienced by those who grow only by adding members from the church roster.

Remember, "The harvest is plentiful..." (Matthew 9:37).

8. Avoid promoting groups as the place of perfect community.

Participants will be in for certain disappointment if they are led to believe that cell groups will always provide a place of ultimate community, where lifelong friends will be developed in a problem-free environment. Authentic cell groups definitely provide powerful and life-changing experiences, but the groups are full of imperfect people who are still on the Christian journey.

Henri Nouwen describes this kind of powerful but imperfect community: "Nothing is sweet or easy about community. Community is a fellowship of people who do not hide their joys and sorrows but make them visible to each other in a gesture of hope. In community we say: 'Life is full of gains and losses, joys and sorrows, ups and downs—but we do not have to live it alone. We want to drink our cup together and thus celebrate the truth that the wounds of our individual lives, which seem intolerable when lived alone, become sources of healing when we live them as part of a fellowship of mutual care.'"[8] The vision for a small-group ministry should avoid leading people to believe that they'll discover a Christian utopia. All authentic group experiences will be a combination of conflict and agreement, anger and sadness, boredom and enthusiasm. Some groups even form cliques within themselves, which of course can be painful for those who don't feel they are a significant part.

The vision for a small-group ministry should avoid leading people to believe that they'll discover Christian utopia. All authentic group experiences will be a combination of conflict and agreement, anger and sadness, boredom and enthusiasm.

9. Don't limit Gen X groups to just Gen Xers.

In his book *Generating Hope: A Strategy for Reaching the Postmodern Generation,* Jimmy Long suggests that "Many Christians are succumbing to the postmodern temptation to fragment or tribalize into smaller units within the church. God does want us to be involved in smaller communities. However, when those smaller communities become tribal groups, we are in danger of fragmenting. Tribal groups are groups through which we gain identity and to which we give loyalty, even to the exclusion of the larger group." [9]

For many years we divided our groups into younger singles, mature singles, and marrieds. We eventually realized we'd created unhealthy divisions. People in different life stages have much to share with one another and, more often than not, want to be in community together. When single and married people participate in the same group, they can learn from one another and be energized. When young members are mixed with mature participants, the experience is characteristically a healthy mixture of both wisdom and idealism.

Gen Xers generally don't like to be segmented or marginalized. They want to be a vital part of the broader community of age, life stage, gender, culture, and ethnicity. Creating a mixed environment can definitely be a source of tension, but handled with care, it can provide a wealth of life-changing experiences.

10. Provide helpful resources, but don't promote a regimented agenda.

The beauty of published curriculum is that someone else has already done the work of preparing group study material. Gen X cell-group leaders should be encouraged to use resources that promote active learning but should avoid those that consistently require a regimented lesson or agenda. As I suggested earlier, an authentic group experience is one that is flexible and allows opportunities for the Holy Spirit to work.

Cell-group curriculum resources should be researched and chosen based on specific needs rather than selected because of convenience.

Gen X cell-group leaders should be encouraged to use resources that promote active learning but to avoid those that consistently require a regimented lesson or agenda.

This Hour Belongs to Generation X

For the church to effectively reach Generation X today, there must be opportunities for both personal solitude and participation in authentic Christ-centered cell groups. Balancing the two is essential, as Dietrich Bonhoeffer notes: "Each by itself has profound pitfalls and perils. Anyone who wants fellowship without solitude plunges into the void of words and feelings, and one who seeks solitude without fellowship perishes in the abyss of vanity, self-infatuation, and despair. Let him who cannot be alone beware of community. Let him who is not in community beware of being alone." [10]

Providing opportunities for authentic community is the primary key to reaching the heart of Generation X. Since Xers will be the next leaders to carry on the work of Christ through the church, whatever effort it takes to provide them with opportunities for life-changing spiritual formation is well worth it.

One author puts it this way, "The call of the wild upon Generation X is awesome. It is a high calling that will require all the intellect, creativity, hope, love, and imagination God provides. The fruit of the Holy Spirit is the equipment for this great challenge, and the body of Christ is the family through which this calling will be fulfilled. The world waits. The devout Muslims, the urban poor, the abused youth, the embattled ethnic minorities, the ravaged earth, the post-Christian society. They wait…This hour belongs to Generation X—and the Lord is calling." [11]

Endnotes

1. Tom Beaudoin, *Virtual Faith: The Irreverent Spiritual Quest of Generation X* (San Francisco, CA: Jossey-Bass Publishers, 1998), 52.

2. Beaudoin, *Virtual Faith: The Irreverent Spiritual Quest of Generation X,* 95.

3. Thomas Bender, *Community and Social Change in America* (Baltimore, MD: John Hopkins University Press, 1978), 6.

4. Gordon Alexander and Douglas G. Alexander, *Biology* (New York, NY: Harper and Row Publishers, 1970), 27.

5. Darrell L. Guder, ed., *Missional Church: A Vision for the Sending of the Church in North America* (Grand Rapids, MI: William B. Eerdmans Publishing Company, 1998), 148-149.

6. Beaudoin, *Virtual Faith: The Irreverent Spiritual Quest of Generation X,* 74.

7. Henri J.M. Nouwen, *In the Name of Jesus: Reflections on Christian Leadership* (New York, NY: Crossroad Publishing, 1989), 44-45.

8. Henri J.M. Nouwen, *Can You Drink the Cup?* (Notre Dame, IN: Ave Maria Press, 1996), 57.

9. Jimmy Long, *Generating Hope: A Strategy for Reaching the Postmodern Generation* (Downers Grove, IL: InterVarsity Press, 1997), 97.

10. Dietrich Bonhoeffer, *Life Together* (New York, NY: Harper and Row, 1954), 78.

11. Dan Harrison with Gordon Aeschliman, *Romancing the Globe: The Call of the Wild on Generation X* (Downers Grove, IL: InterVarsity Press, 1993), 80.

CHAPTER 5

Unleashing Small-Group Power

STEVE R. SHEELEY

Steve Sheeley is an experienced small-group administrator and a prolific writer on the subject of small-group ministry. Steve and his wife, Marla, recently pioneered a hybrid church, incorporating small-group dynamics into the whole church.

Creating Small-Group Experiences Throughout Your Church

The stories are breathtaking. A small-group meets in a hospital room as a member recovers from a mastectomy Another small group huddles around a couple who have just lost a child. "I never knew church could be so powerful," says one person; "I go to church, but my small group is where church happens for me," says another. The meeting starts with prayer. Soon it becomes holy ground. Friends are made, hearts are opened, Scriptures are applied, and lives are changed. A special power is unleashed in a small-group setting, the power of love.

The life-changing power of small groups is so significant, in fact, that it raises some serious questions: Why are these wonderful experiences limited to small groups? Why is one of the most profound, life-changing opportunities a church can offer experienced by a small part of the congregation? Why do small-group experiences differ so much from the other opportunities churches offer? Why was there a need to begin with for a small-group movement where people could experience what the church should have been offering all along?

While there are no simple answers, one thing is certain: The success of the small-group movement has shown that people are aching to share their hearts and lives with one another.

While there are no simple answers, one thing is certain: The success of the small-group movement has shown that people are aching to share their hearts and lives with one another.

Since the first-century church experienced a level of group intimacy that was very rich, one more question must be added to the list: What happened to the modern church? While there are as many answers to this question as there are theologians, for the purposes of this chapter, I will share two significant observations:

1. We live in a culture that resists intimate personal contact.

People today live in anonymous communities. We don't know our neighbors, and our closest friends are our co-workers. We huddle inside our homes and watch television, build anonymous relationships on the Internet, and sit in our cars listening to voices on the radio.

The human interaction we have outside our homes is friendly and polite, but it hardly makes a dent in the surface of what human beings are really capable of. Unfortunately, the trend toward avoiding intimate personal contact has permeated our churches. People arrive at church and leave again, often without even speaking to each other.

2. Churches have adopted institutional models of ministry.

In addition to acquiescing to the contemporary phenomenon known as cocooning, many churches have adopted the characteristics of academic institutions. Seminaries today are caught in a conflict between academic excellence and vocational relevance. For many seminaries and divinity schools, the temptation to be like graduate schools rather than professional schools is quite alluring.

When ministers are trained in academic environments that emphasize scholarly approaches to theology, hermeneutics, and ecclesiology, it shouldn't be surprising that today's churches are taking on the qualities of educational institutions.

When ministers are trained in academic environments that emphasize scholarly approaches to theology, hermeneutics, and ecclesiology, it shouldn't be surprising that today's churches are taking on the qualities of educational institutions. Certainly, churches are supposed to be places of learning, but there is certain danger in adopting an institutional or academic model to understand and carry out ministry. Compassion, trust, and intimacy are each priceless parts of the church experience but are often inconsistent with academia.

Rudiments of the academic setting can often be observed in the worship experiences of many churches. The most obvious can be seen in congregations whose worshipers are characterized as passive spectators. A worship service that is limited to the contribution of only a few participants makes a significant statement about the values of a church. Just because a church attracts a large number of participants and appears to be growing doesn't guarantee an intimate community life.

The reasons why many congregations today lack a sense of intimate community are not nearly as important as understanding how they can get back to a model closer to that of the first-century church. The initial consideration is actually simpler than it might first appear. Why not incorporate the life-changing power of small groups into the whole church rather than limiting them only to a small-group setting?

In a sense, small-group ministries today are an indictment against the larger church's ability to provide life-changing results in people's lives. Even if a particular congregation supports small-group ministry as a tool to foster intimate, caring relationships, if it doesn't actively value these relationships throughout the whole church, the small-group ministry itself will be limited in its overall effect. The polarization that can result between a small-group ministry and a passive, nonrelational church can, over time, corrupt the potential of a small-group. This is significant in understanding why so many small-group ministries have failed in the past decade. Small groups that take root in this kind of setting will eventually disconnect from the life of the church and degenerate into self-serving entities. Because a group's potential to maintain healthy interpersonal relationships is significantly restricted in this kind of setting, potential for a long-term existence is diminished.

Whether or not a congregation decides to maintain a small-group ministry, it's imperative that the church as a whole become a place that offers a variety of opportunities for dramatic life-changing results.

> *Even if a particular congregation supports small-group ministry as a tool to foster intimate, caring relationships, if it doesn't actively value these relationships throughout the whole church, the small-group ministry itself will be limited in its overall effect.*

> *In a sense, small-group ministries today are an indictment against the larger church's ability to provide life-changing results in people's lives.*

Fifteen Characteristics of a Life-Changing Church

There are fifteen characteristics that, in one form or another, provide the backbone for a successful small-group ministry. These characteristics give small groups the impetus to be significant in the lives of people. They aren't original by any means. Each one has a solid biblical foundation and can be attributed to the New Testament church. This first-century church experienced a level of group intimacy that is very close to that of today's small-group experience. But it was an intimacy that wasn't limited to a particular setting or group of people; it permeated the entire church. For a congregation to be life-changing beyond its small-group ministry, these characteristics need to be present in the fuller life of the church as well.

Each of the fifteen characteristics, as introduced on the next few pages, is followed by questions designed to provide a needs assessment as a tool to appraise a congregation's potential to have a positive, life-changing impact on its members. The needs assessment can actually be utilized in two ways:

1. to appraise a congregation's potential to have a positive, life-changing impact on its members; and

2. to assess the effectiveness of a small-group ministry.

Following each question, space has been provided for writing a few thoughts as you consider the characteristics and how they apply to your particular situation. While the needs assessment is provided primarily to assess the overall congregational experience, it's also a very helpful tool to use in evaluating the effectiveness of a small-group ministry. The answers to the questions will indicate a congregation's strengths and weaknesses and will provide insight into areas that need further development.

CONGREGATIONAL AND SMALL-GROUP NEEDS ASSESSMENT SURVEY

1. Encouragement

In the first-century church, a member's exemplary Christian behavior was typically affirmed when members gathered, either formally or socially. The New Testament contains many examples of affirmation and encouragement, including, among others, Paul's affirmation of Epaphras in Colossians 4:12-13. These New Testament affirmations went beyond the typical social affirmations often heard in churches today, such as, "That outfit looks nice on you." They were given for Christlike behavior, taking the form of such affirmations as, "That was a very Christlike thing that you did," or "You reminded me of Jesus when you continued to offer respect to that person even though she ridiculed your faith."

The model of encouragement found in the New Testament is one that affirmed members in their relationships with God in ways that reminded them what was truly important (1 Thessalonians 4:13-18, 5:11; Hebrews 3:13, 10:25). To have a life-changing impact on its members, a church must model that same type of encouragement and remind people about what's really important in their lives.

Questions for Assessment

• Do your leaders publicly affirm the Christlikeness of others? If so, in what ways?

_____

_____

_____

• How are the volunteers who play the organ, clean the sanctuary, mow the lawn, provide nursery care, and do other thankless jobs recognized and encouraged for what they contribute to God's purposes and the life of the church?

_____

_____

_____

    • Are opportunities for members to affirm one another included in church gatherings? If so, which gatherings, and how is affirmation facilitated?

_____

_____

_____

    • Do the staff and other church leadership model this characteristic by encouraging one another? If so, in what ways?

_____

_____

_____

2. Active Participation

Despite the size of the church gatherings in the New Testament,[1] Christians who had received the Holy Spirit were invited to make contributions to the gathering. Paul's words to the Corinthian Christians illustrated this when he said, "When you come together, everyone has a hymn, a word of instruction, a revelation, a tongue, or an interpretation. All of these must be done for the strengthening of the church" (1 Corinthians 14:26).

For the whole congregation to have the life-changing impact of a small group, regardless of worship style or tradition, there should be opportunities for active and interactive participation. Corporate contribution and interaction in worship and other church programs are vital for several reasons: (1) It values the giftedness of each participant; (2) it makes worship more meaningful and memorable; and (3) it broadens understanding and give participants new perspective.

Active participation is what gives life-changing power to the small-group experience and makes it memorable. These same experiences can become part of almost any church setting or program.

Questions for Assessment

• What are the specific activities that provide opportunities for participants to become actively involved in worship?

_____

_____

• How is input from members encouraged as a part of worship planning and music selection?

_____

_____

• What methods are used to invite church members to preach, sing, pray, and share in a worship service?

_____

_____

3. Corporate Prayer

In the early New Testament church, opportunities were frequently provided for Christians to share personal concerns that would be included in corporate prayer. (For some examples, see Romans 15:31; Ephesians 6:18-20; Colossians 4:3-4; and 2 Thessalonians 3:1-2.) These prayer concerns went beyond comforting the afflicted and were devoted to fulfilling God's purposes in a person's life.[2] Opportunities to share meaningful prayer concerns are usually present in a small-group setting and should be extended into the whole life of the church.

Questions for Assessment

• What opportunities are offered for shared prayer concerns in church gatherings? Are the shared concerns actually prayed for? If so, by whom?

_____

_____

• In what ways are those prayer concerns communicated to the wider body of believers in the congregation?

_____

_____

_____

4. Open Communication and Conflict Resolution

Not only is conflict resolution an important part of small-group life, but it was definitely a trademark of the early church. Peter and Paul, for example, had their differences, but Scripture suggests they dealt with their disagreements in a straightforward manner and without speaking harshly to one another (Galatians 2:11-14). This level of resolution is possible only in an environment where Christ's love is the true foundation of all relationships. When confrontation does become necessary, a congregation, just like a small group, must seek to provide a loving environment where trust supercedes all human agendas and where there is little fear of relational damage.

One of the most effective ways for minimizing conflict is by providing an environment where healthy dialogue can take place. This includes opportunities for feedback on sermons, lessons, and programs.

Questions for Assessment

• How are conflicts resolved at your church?

_____

_____

_____

• In what ways do congregational leaders model conflict resolution?

_____

_____

_____

• What opportunities are there to teach church members about healthy conflict resolution?

_____

_____

_____

• If someone grumbles or gossips in a manner that has a negative effect on the congregation, how is that person confronted about his or her behavior?

_____

_____

_____

• What opportunities does your church provide for members to respond to sermons, lessons, and programs?

_____

_____

_____

• How does your church equip members to practice effective listening skills with one another?

_____

_____

_____

5. Emphasis on Personal Transformation

Personal transformation was a characteristic woven deeply into the early church. This transformation took a variety of forms, including close relationships with other believers, a solid sense of belonging, moral accountability, praying together, sharing, and trust. Considering the combined power of these elements, it shouldn't be surprising that so many people experienced radical personal transformation. In a sense, this meant that the church wasn't afraid to roll up its sleeves and get its hands dirty. People came into Christian gatherings with painful baggage and troubled lives. They relied heavily on one another as they turned away from harmful behavior that had become deeply engrained in their lives. They groaned and wept as they laid their lives before Christ. Personal transformation was significant, and the early church didn't flinch when someone came to Christ looking to be rescued.[3] There was always an expectation that both new and veteran Christians would continue to experience transformation and growth in their lives.[4] Just as it was in the early church, personal transformation is a hallmark of successful small groups and is a necessary characteristic for a church to be truly life-changing.

Questions for Assessment

• In what ways are unchurched guests and seekers challenged to accept Christ and make a confession of faith? As a result, how many people joined your church last year by accepting Christ as their Lord and Savior?

_____

_____

_____

• What discipleship programs does your congregation have in place to guide new Christians through an initial encounter with Christ?

_____

_____

_____

• How have church members been trained to guide new believers through an initial confession of faith?

_____

_____

_____

• How would the members of your congregation react if a person with a notorious lifestyle responded positively and accepted Christ during a worship service?

_____

_____

_____

6. Trusting Environment

Early New Testament Christians invested very deeply in their relationships with one another.[5] As a result, they generated significant trust, which allowed these Christians many opportunities to share their true feelings and emotions with each other. The New Testament provides several examples of believers sharing tears, anger, fear, shame, contrition, and joy. Paul instructed them to "rejoice with those who rejoice; mourn with those who mourn" (Romans 12:15).

Successful small groups provide an atmosphere that allows for emotional sharing and expression among participants. In the same way, for a congregation to flourish on a deeply relational level, as the early church did, it should provide ways, other than a small-group ministry, to encourage trusting connections among church members.

Questions for Assessment

• Other than small groups, what does your church do to encourage personal trusting connections among members?

_____

_____

_____

• Does your church provide a safe environment for people to express their feelings? Why or why not?

_____

_____

_____

• Use the following scale to rate the trust level of your congregation, with 10 representing the highest trust level.

1	2	3	4	5	6	7	8	9	10
Low Level of Trust								High Level of Trust	

• Why did you rate the trust level as you did?

_____

_____

_____

7. Opportunities for Ministry

Since New Testament Christians were endowed with spiritual gifts as a result of receiving the Holy Spirit, opportunities to share their gifts were encouraged (1 Corinthians 12:1-31). If a person demonstrated the gift of patience or encouragement, his or her ability was acknowledged and given opportunities for fruitful expression. If another person had the gift of administration, he or she was placed in a position to use the gift for God's glory (Romans 12:4-8). Similarly, specific roles in the church, such as pastor and evangelist, were identified based on the spiritual gifts of a church member (Ephesians 4:11-13; 1 Corinthians 12:27-31). This early ministry model clearly illustrates that church membership means more than just a casual association with other Christians; membership implies that a member will actively engage in a ministry based on his or her spiritual gifts.

Questions for Assessment

• What percentage of your church membership is involved in an active ministry of some type?

_____

_____

_____

• What are some of the obstacles that keep this from being a higher percentage?

_____

_____

_____

• What is your congregation's expectation that each new member will utilize his or her gifts in ministry?

_____

_____

_____

• How are members encouraged to get actively involved in ministry?

_____

_____

_____

• How does your church help members identify their spiritual gifts and talents?

_____

_____

_____

• How often do ministers come from within the congregation, and in what ways are members encouraged to consider active involvement in pastoral ministry?

_____

_____

_____

8. Setting an Example

Valuable resources for the New Testament church were the many Christians who set patterns for living that were worth emulating. It was important for leaders to have those whom they could point to as examples of faithful living (1 Corinthians 11:1; Philippians 3:17). In his second letter to the Thessalonians Paul reminds Christians to set examples for others to follow (2 Thessalonians 3:7-10).

In a time of history where heroes and significant role models are infrequent, it is important for the modern church to have examples of those living a life of faith worth imitating. This characteristic applies not only to small-group ministry but to both the local congregation and the church at large.

Questions for Assessment

• Identify some recent examples of church members who were publicly identified and praised as worthy of imitation.

_____

_____

_____

NEEDS ASSESSMENT SURVEY

• What methods are used to encourage members to set living examples?

_____

_____

9. Family Friendly

The New Testament church provided a safe family environment to all those who joined the Christian fellowship. Various words such as "sister" (Romans 16:1), "brother" (Acts 9:17; Romans 14:15), and "mother" (1 Thessalonians 2:7; Romans 16:13) were used to describe a few of the surrogate family roles that Christians played in the lives of one another. For many people, especially the disconnected, the church became a family-of-choice.[6] It's also interesting to note that the New Testament provides more Scripture passages referring to church members as family than it does to biological families.

A small-group ministry typically provides an environment where Christians can be nurtured in family-friendly love and trust; but like the other characteristics, a family-friendly environment must permeate the entire church. To be significant in the lives of people today, congregations must provide environments for people without families to receive care as well as opportunities for established families to become more deeply involved in each other's lives.

Questions for Assessment

• Would members of your congregation describe their relationships with one another as familylike? Why or why not?

_____

_____

• Do other church members celebrate key events in members' lives, such as holidays, births, promotions, funerals, and weddings? If so, in what ways?

_____

_____

• What activities does your church specifically provide that would fall under the category of family ministry?

_____

_____

_____

• In what ways does your church provide love and support for members who don't have immediate connections to biological families, such as widows, orphans, and homeless people?

_____

_____

_____

10. Intergenerational Interaction

The New Testament acknowledges the value of intergenerational interaction and the importance of sharing wisdom with one another (Titus 2:1-6). In his letter to the Galatians Paul said, "you are all one in Christ Jesus" (Galatians 3:28). We can understand this to mean that all people are important to Jesus Christ, no matter what ethnic background, social status, or age. Jesus himself also acknowledged the importance of children as part of God's kingdom (Matthew 18:1-6). It's very easy to make a biblical case for the importance of intergenerational interaction in the New Testament church. This applies to both small groups and the larger congregation. While it often takes more work to form cross-sectional groups, the experiences are richer as participants share from various perspectives.

Questions for Assessment

• What steps has your church taken to create and maintain intergenerational groups?

_____

_____

_____

• How are people of different lifestyles and backgrounds encouraged to interact?

_____

_____

_____

• What do you perceive to be the benefits of intergenerational programming in your congregation?

_____

_____

_____

11. Unity

Care was taken in the early church to ensure that every believer shared a common understanding of those aspects of the Christian faith that were most important (1 Corinthians 1:10; Philippians 2:1-2). Organizational unity was not based on heritage, social status, or income, but on belief in Christ. In fact, unity among these early Christians was so important that even atrocious conditions, such as slavery, were secondary to being united in faith through Christ.[7] Unity was also apparent in the way early Christians talked freely about their belief in Christ as compared to those who didn't (1 Corinthians 6:6; 1 Thessalonians 4:11-12). Openly articulating faith boundaries helped to build group unity in the early church and reminded members of their purpose together.

Questions for Assessment

• Besides worshiping together, what other congregational activities help establish a group identity?

_____

_____

• What does your church leadership do to develop a sense of unity among members?

_____

_____

• What efforts are made to improve the quality of the relationships church members share with one another?

_____

_____

_____

12. Need Sharing

In the New Testament church, there was no shame in members' acknowledging personal needs. Need-sharing was an intrinsic part of the life of the church.[8] Requests such as "I need prayer for a temptation I am facing" or "We are struggling financially and need food" were both common and appropriate during gatherings (Acts 2:44-45; 2 Corinthians 9:6-15; Ephesians 4:29; James 2:16). The early church chose to practice selfless generosity in a form that closely resembled the lifestyle of Jesus and his disciples.

Questions for Assessment

• In what ways are church members invited to safely share their needs with one another?

_____

_____

_____

• How does your church respond to these needs?

_____

_____

_____

13. Hospitality

The friendships and closeness that early Christians enjoyed together didn't stop when a formal church gathering ended. They encouraged each other and interacted socially throughout the rest of the week (Hebrews 3:13). Hospitality was a valued ministry during the early church.[9] These early Christians were encouraged to invite one another into their lives and homes.

Today, relationship-building and hospitality are at the core of the small-group experience and should also be practiced throughout the entire congregation.

Questions for Assessment

• What does your church do to encourage expressions of hospitality throughout the week?

_____

_____

• How do members stay in contact with each other when away from formal church events?

_____

_____

14. Declaration of Faith and Confession

The early church recognized the value of believers making public professions of their faith in Christ, such as "Jesus is Lord" (Romans 10:9). Just as it is today, hearing a new member make a faith declaration was undoubtedly a very powerful experience in the New Testament church.

Public confession was also important in the New Testament church because it demonstrated an individual's honesty about personal sin, acknowledged the need for God's grace, and allowed opportunities for spiritual healing (James 5:16; 1 John 1:9).

It goes without saying that opportunities for confession and public declarations of faith should be present in the small-group setting as well as the larger church.

Questions for Assessment

• What opportunities does your church provide for new members to profess their faith in Christ?

_____

_____

• How is confession encouraged and modeled in your congregation?

_____

_____

• How would your church members react if a minister or pastor confessed a sin during a Sunday morning worship service?

_____

_____

_____

15. Evangelism

In the New Testament church, apostles and church leaders were very articulate in sharing their faith stories with others (Acts 22:1-21, 26:2-32; Philippians 1:12-30). These stories were offered, not only because they were dramatic and life changing, but because they were especially important in leading non-Christians to Christ. In the same way, sharing faith stories today provides an important ingredient for evangelism in both the small-group and church setting.

Questions for Assessment

• How do leaders model faith sharing in your congregation?

_____

_____

_____

• In what ways are members actively involved in evangelism and sharing their faith stories?

_____

_____

_____

• What methods are used to teach church members the importance of evangelism and faith sharing?

_____

_____

_____

NEEDS ASSESSMENT SURVEY

Summarizing the Assessment

• Which of the fifteen characteristics did you discover to be the strengths of your congregation (or small group)?

_____

_____

_____

_____

• Which did you discover were the weakest?

_____

_____

_____

_____

• How would your church be different if all these characteristics were a vital part of your congregation?

_____

_____

_____

• How would visitors and seekers experience your church?

_____

_____

_____

• Which of the characteristics would be easiest to integrate into your church right now? Why?

_____

_____

_____

• Which would be the most difficult to integrate right now? Why?

_____

_____

_____

Integrating the Characteristics Into the Life of the Church

For most church leaders, the fifteen characteristics will seem obvious for any church to be vital in today's culture. Unfortunately, many of them are conspicuously missing from the life of a large percentage of congregations.

As we have briefly observed, these characteristics formed the backbone of the New Testament church and gave it impetus to have life-changing impact in the lives of early Christians. The success or failure of small groups today typically can be attributed to the presence or absence of these characteristics. In the same way, integrating them into the life of a congregation will allow it to become a place where dramatic, life-changing occurrences are commonplace rather than rare.

Indeed, it is the power of Jesus Christ and the Holy Spirit that actually transforms people, but these characteristics provide the tools through which Christ works.

Indeed, it is the power of Jesus Christ and the Holy Spirit that actually transforms people, but these characteristics provide the tools through which Christ works.

Here are a few suggestions to help incorporate the intimate experiences of a small-group environment into the whole life of the church.

Leader support. It goes without saying that the leadership has tremendous influence on the life of a congregation. The influence, either positive or negative, depends on what the leaders themselves value. If the leadership predominately comes from an institutional or academic background, the church may very well be operating on an institutional model for ministry. This of course means that programs and organization will typically take a higher priority than the development of intimate relationships. While it may be the most difficult of the potential obstacles to overcome, support of congregational leadership is the primary key to creating a

While it may be the most difficult of the potential obstacles to overcome, support of congregational leadership is the primary key to creating a relevant, life-changing church.

relevant, life-changing church.

While there is no easy way to convince passive or resistant leaders of the necessity of taking steps to revitalize the congregation, having them work through the characteristic needs assessment will be a helpful place to begin.

Articulating the vision. Once leaders are supportive, they must articulate the vision to the entire congregation. The vision can be articulated in any of several ways. A good place to begin is through a sermon or teaching series covering each of the fifteen characteristics of a transformational church. For a congregation to get behind an idea, it's vital that its members be fully educated and informed from the inception.

Obtaining feedback. Once the vision has been cast to the congregation, it's important to give them opportunities for feedback and input. Providing these kinds of opportunities is important for several reasons: (1) Church leaders will have a constructive opportunity to clarify and respond to concerns and questions; (2) input from the congregation often brings new ideas and approaches that leaders didn't consider; and (3) the environment of trust and affirmation that will develop through opportunities for open feedback will demonstrate that the leadership is serious about becoming a transformational church.

The environment of trust and affirmation that will begin to develop through opportunities for open feedback will demonstrate that the leadership is serious about becoming a transformational church.

Taking small steps. Too many changes too rapidly can put fear into the heart of the most open-minded member. Thus, an essential key to a successful transformation is to start small.

After receiving feedback from the congregation, the next step is to develop a step-by-step plan. The answers you provided on the needs assessment will indicate which specific areas should be addressed. The best place to begin is by integrating those characteristics into the life of the congregation that will be confronted by the fewest obstacles. A few immediate successes will motivate church leaders and members to push toward the final goal.

Integrating activities. It would be difficult to include every single characteristic in any one setting. But every activity in the church can be assessed to see which characteristics are already present and which need to be incorporated. There are always opportunities to expand and improve existing programs and ministries. Some of these opportunities include Sunday school, children's programs, youth events, family and intergenerational activities, committee or board meetings, staff meetings, leadership training events, retreats, and small groups.

Worship services deserve special attention because worship offers a good environment for intimacy and personal transformation. The primary question to ask of worship is "How can it be made to demonstrate the value a congregation places on personal transformation?" The order of worship service should never become more important than the congregation's need to experience intimacy and relevance. Members and guests must all find opportunities to become actively involved in the worship experience. This means more than sitting, praying quietly, listening, and singing an occasional hymn.

There are many activities that can be included in worship that will actively engage the congregation in the worship experience; for example,

• Open the floor for prayer concerns and joys from the congregation;

• Allow opportunities for members to share their faith stories;

• Allow worshipers to ask questions, discuss faith issues, and provide feedback to sermons;

• Publicly affirm and recognize the giftedness of church members;

• Provide an opportunity after the worship service for people to remain and engage in dialogue or ask questions about the sermon;

• Take an offering and give the proceeds to needy church members;

• Provide small groups opportunities to share what is happening in their group;

• Provide new believers with an opportunity to make public declarations of faith;

• Invite members to be actively involved in planning worship;

• Encourage worshipers to get into groups, share prayer needs, and pray for one another;

A s with any new activity, be sure to allow opportunities for evaluation and feedback to ensure it's having the effect that was initially intended.

• Provide opportunities for children and youth to be actively involved in worship.

The possibilities are limited only by the creativity of those who plan worship. As with any new activity, however, be sure to allow opportunities for evaluation and feedback to ensure it's having the effect that was initially intended.

Starting new programs. In order to incorporate some of the characteristics, a congregation may have to start some new programs or ministries. These might include such things as starting a mentoring program that pairs mature Christians with new Christians; utilizing a spiritual gifts assessment to help members evaluate their gifts, talents, and abilities and then providing them with specific ministry opportunities; starting an intergenerational program where people have dinner together and discuss relevant topics; offering brief, one-session training classes on listening skills, praying, and conflict resolution; and beginning a family heritage-building program or starting a midweek program with a small-group emphasis, such as Group Publishing's Faith Weaver™ midweek program (available fall of 2000).

A small-group ministry should be established not to replace other intimate life-changing opportunities within the congregation but as a microcosm of what is happening throughout the whole church.

Starting a small-group ministry. Once you've laid the groundwork for an environment of personal transformation throughout the congregation, if you haven't already done so, it's time to start a small-group ministry. Establishing small groups within a congregation that values personal transformation will result in tremendous success.

Small-group leaders should be trained to understand the characteristics that provide the impetus for a life-changing group. A small-group ministry should be established not to replace other intimate life-changing opportunities within the congregation but as a microcosm of what is occurring throughout the whole church.

A Place of Personal Transformation

Becoming a church that has integrated the life-changing power of a small group is a formidable task. The results, however, will be worth the effort. When a church is committed to being a place for personal transformation instead of talking and singing about God, it will become a place that demonstrates the power and presence of God. Just as medieval Gothic architecture revealed God's transcendence and majesty, a transformational church reveals evidence of God's grace to the world.

> *When a church is committed to being a place of personal transformation instead of talking and singing about God, it will become a place that demonstrates the power and presence of God.*

Unleashing the life-changing power of a small group throughout a congregation will frighten some members. There will always be those who are uncomfortable with a church that encourages and expects personal intimacy and life-changing encounters with God. But there is no reason to apologize for becoming like the New Testament church. Jesus himself was constantly engaged in leading people toward personal transformation. The challenge for the church today is to do the same. When this happens, a special power will be unleashed—the power of love!

Endnotes

1. Estimates of the square footage of the dining areas in the homes of wealthy Corinthians suggest that the maximum size of the gatherings was around fifty people. See Abraham Malherbe, *Social Aspects of Early Christianity* (Philadelphia, PA: Fortress Press, 1983) 73-74 and Robert Banks, *Paul's Idea of Community* (Grand Rapids, MI: William B. Eerdman's Publishing, 1988) 41.

2. Instead of simply praying for Aunt Martha's arthritis, for example, people prayed for healing with the hope that Aunt Martha would observe the power of God and make a confession of faith. Or they prayed that being healed would free Aunt Martha to return to her life of proclaiming and demonstrating the Kingdom of God. Paul's prayer in the first chapter of Colossians is an example of this.

3. See 1 Corinthians 14:24-25. Paul's description of an unbeliever reacting to a powerful, relational church gathering is evidence of the confession and emotional expression a church is capable of accommodating.

4. Consider Paul himself. He spoke often about who he was before Christ and who he is becoming since his encounter with Jesus. Since Paul was responsible for starting many in the churches who received the epistles, there is no doubt that Paul himself established a precedent of these churches as places of radical personal transformation.

5. Paul's goodbye to the Ephesians elders in Acts 20:16–21:1 is a touching example of this.

6. 1 Peter, 1 Corinthians 1:18-31 and Ephesians 2:19–22 all suggest that the first churches included believers who were disenfranchised from traditional sources of love and belonging.

7. Paul's letter to Philemon, the owner of the slave Onesimus, is not an appeal for abolition; it is an appeal for friendship and submission to God's purposes. Similarly, the epistle writers never made an issue out of slavery, but they encouraged slaves and slave owners to glorify Christ in their roles.

8. Churches described in the New Testament met one another's needs in light of a new life in Christ that ultimately resulted in a powerful, spirit-filled life. Needs were met in order that this new life could be realized.

9. The intimacy experienced in these churches indicates that hospitality was practiced among church members (3 John 1:6-8). In addition, the early church relied heavily on itinerant teachers, prophets, and evangelists who needed inexpensive lodging and were typically offered hospitality from fellow Christians. (See Romans 12:13 and 1 Peter 4:9.)

CHAPTER 6
Integrating Sunday Schools as Small Groups

CARL F. GEORGE

Carl George is a prolific writer and well-known small-group and church growth expert. He has conducted a variety of national training events and currently serves as a consultant to various churches and associations worldwide.

Don't overlook the obvious!

In the late 1800s, Russell Conwell, a Philadelphia preacher, founded Temple University. To help raise money for it, he preached over six thousand times, using a story that became a classic. In his "Acres of Diamonds" sermon, Conwell tells the story of a man who gives up everything to pursue his dream of discovering a treasure trove of diamonds. After his death, the diamonds that eluded him were found—in his own back yard!

In the same way, church leaders sometimes decide to strike out to organize brand new small groups. They promote these groups because they want others to share in the warmth and sense of community that comes from a small-group experience. What they fail to see, however, is that many ready opportunities already exist—in their Sunday school classes.

One church I knew had a minister on staff who was assigned to oversee the small-group ministry. He took an old closet and turned it into a war room. On one wall he mapped all the meetings of the church, by leader and location. On another wall, he listed all the new small groups he hoped to start. Month after month, the number of new groups he was trying to launch remained at less than a dozen. But during the same time, more than fifty established groups or classes were holding meetings every week. It never occurred to him to look at all those existing classes as potential small groups. Since many of them were labeled "Sunday school classes," he didn't consider them as having small-group potential. As a result, he never approached class leaders to help them make their classes function more relationally, as small groups do.

> *It never occurred to him to look at all those existing classes as potential small groups.*

When you hear "Sunday school," why don't you think "small group"?

Suppose you spent the early years of your Christian life attending only a worship service. You'd probably start thinking that church was only about that one big meeting. If someone organized a Sunday school and invited you to attend, you'd obviously recognize it as a smaller group than the worship service. You'd discover that you could do things in the smaller class that you couldn't do in the bigger meeting, such as ask questions whenever they popped into your head. You'd discover that you could share your feelings about a subject and even have the group stop and focus on your needs. You'd probably discover a lay person serving as the group leader instead of a professional clergy person. In a small meeting, you couldn't hide very well, but you probably wouldn't want to either.

The reality is that most of us did not begin our Christian lives in a church with only a worship service. We started in a church with much more, including clergy, elders, deacons, choirs, ushers, Sunday school classes, men's and women's clubs, children's weekday clubs, youth outings, softball teams, and so forth. One thing most of us learned by experience is that many of these groups didn't deliver the quality of experience that we wanted.

Of course, the logical thing to do when you want something is to go after it wherever you first found it. If you first found quality fellowship in a home-based small group, that's where you'd expect to find it again. Too often, people never think of Sunday schools as having the potential to be intimate small groups.

What's going on in Sunday school that we can get excited about?

Sunday school programs serve different functions in different congregations. Some people see the Sunday school program as little more than quality child care while they are in worship. Others see it as a way to teach kids the basics about religion, like catechism, where they memorize correct answers to the big questions. Most Christian educators recognize the Sunday school program as an easy way to get adult members' attention for an extra hour.

Unfortunately, some small-group workers feel that a Sunday school cannot possibly deliver what a home Bible study or prayer group can. They contend that the feeling is not the same as it is in someone's home. The classroom décor is too barren. The lesson is usually taught from an outline instead of being shared from a life experience. Besides, there is only a short time available on Sunday mornings.

Unfortunately, some small-group workers feel that a Sunday school cannot possibly deliver what a home Bible study or prayer group can.

But the fact remains that in smaller groupings, personal attention can be given to each individual.

Why not turn Sunday schools into effective small-group networks?

You may study as many congregations as you want to. You'll find the most obvious event is the weekly worship service. The second most obvious feature of a typical congregation, regardless of size, is its Sunday school program for children and sometimes for youth and adults. If your desire is to revitalize a church, why start by organizing a new small-group ministry from scratch when you have in your Sunday school program a small-group ministry already organized and waiting for renewal?

If your desire is to revitalize a church, why start by organizing a new small-group ministry from scratch when you have in your Sunday school program a small-group ministry already organized and waiting for renewal?

Not only will the Sunday school program be renewed, but many small-group experiences can be incorporated into these already existing classes.

As I reflect on some emerging trends, it's apparent that some of the ways we categorized church ministry in earlier times are beginning to blur. For example, the distinction between small classes in Sunday school and small groups in homes is often blurred today. Another example of blurring happens between children and adult programs. At one time we thought that our methods and objectives for children were vastly different than those for adults. Today we find

Today we find ourselves needing to look at models where children are being invited to participate in the learning process, not just as students but as mentors, coaches, and operators.

ourselves looking at models where children are being invited to participate in the learning process, not just as students but as mentors, coaches, and operators. Youngsters working alongside adult mentors are doing real jobs.

A new wave of creativity is emerging.

After decades of pursuing excellence in children's Christian education through uniformity and standards, a successful new wave of creativity is beginning to emerge. Inspired in part by Willow Creek Community Church children's programs and a variety of creative church leadership seminars, innovations are being encouraged throughout the land. Many of these ideas involve radical changes, and most are beginning to value intimate relationships through small-group experiences. Of course, this kind of creative ministry calls for the development of bold and innovative leaders.

Of course, this kind of creative ministry calls for the development of bold and innovative leaders.

Join me for a brief flyover of a number of places I have found stimulating.

Byron Baergen, son of Canadian church consultant John and Lorraine Baergen, is an intern with children at the Sherwood Park Christian and Missionary Alliance near Edmonton, Alberta. His ministry team selected several boys and girls in the middle school grades to train as spiritual leaders and tutors for others their own age and younger. These budding leaders are treated with all the respect, training, and attention usually accorded to adult workers in other churches. The kids now see themselves as stewards of their leadership roles, taking learning and leading very seriously.

Down in Cape Girardeau, two hours' drive south of St. Louis, on the Mississippi River, ten-year-old LaCroix United Methodist Church, led by Ron Watts and staff, occupy a new building and rejoice over their newly designed children's facility. From the toddler area built to resemble Noah's Ark to the kindergarten Adventureland with castle-like walls of gray stones, parapets, and coats of arms, the youngsters are transported into another place and time for their learning experiences. Across the hall, a children's auditorium for grades one to four is supported technically by fifth- and sixth-graders who operate lights and a sound system that exceeds most church sanctuaries. Onstage, brightened by theater lights, is a Bible-times mural expertly painted onto backdrop curtains for quick scene changes. Through a doorway, a counseling room beckons with ceiling murals of blue sky and white clouds that are transformed by the onset of night to reveal a glittering Milky Way. While moms and dads sing contemporary songs of praise, their offspring are reveling in biblical lore, entranced by tales of ancient Bible heroes. Staff members have each been charged with building relationships with a select group of children and to act as their guides through the weekly adventures. At appropriate times, they lead their groups into the counseling room for prayer under the starry nightscape. Even more creative than the décor is the job-sharing among a team of five young mothers who each contribute twelve hours a week to mastermind an incredibly creative program that engages their kids in every innovative way.

From the toddler area built to resemble Noah's Ark to the kindergarten Adventureland with castlelike walls of gray stones, parapets, and coats of arms, the youngsters are transported into another place and time for their learning experiences.

Next, fly over eastern Canada to New Brunswick, where in the basement of the Wesleyan Church of Moncton, an otherworldly experience awaits. Promiseland Park, created by the children's ministry team, is set to resemble a garden or park with evergreen trees painted onto the surrounding walls. It's lighted with black light, paved with colored paving stones, and is equipped with seating on real park benches made surreal by daylight fluorescent colors. Children sit in the flood of black light and become part of the scene as they gaze at one another and see their eyes, teeth, and white fabric glow. Seats face a performance area with a "Sesame Street" style puppetville for a backdrop. Live acts and singers come on stage, while puppet masters play out their characters through the windows of the town's structures built into the back wall.

Meanwhile, down in New York City, at Brooklyn's Elim International Church, Carrie Johnson enlists parents and children by pairs into courses on the Bible and theology in an adult/child Bible seminary.

Meanwhile, down in New York City, at Brooklyn's Elim International Church, Carrie Johnson enlists parents and children by pairs into courses on the Bible and theology in an adult/child Bible seminary. She has dual classrooms set up, one for parents and another for children, in which the same text and topics are taught at age-appropriate levels. Each class includes homework projects that involve discussions between parents and their enrolled children. Carrie's concepts work well as midweek or weekend electives, whether scheduled during the Sunday school hour or not.

Before we finish our trip, fly with me over to Chino Hills, California, close to my home, where a rented high school building houses the worship services of the eight-year-old Inland Hills Church. Children's minister Cindy Gonzales oversees a program where hundreds of kids are tented in the courtyard of the school because school authorities will allow the church to use only a few rooms in addition to the auditorium where worship services are held. To make it easy for the children to find their classes, animal figures readily recognizable by the children themselves have been painted on sandwich-board signs. Each age group has its own zoo animal displayed near the rooms or tents occupied by groups of various ages in what is advertised as "Wild Kingdom at IHC." Cindy drives about the plaza in a battery-operated golf cart, consistent with the mode of travel preferred by the staff of local zoos. She has added a pith helmet and bullet bandoleer to round out the costume. The kids love it. They have organized teams of volunteers to do most of the work. Inland Hills Church has grown to a weekly attendance of over twelve hundred participants. The congregation struggles every week for the space and staff it needs. At the same time, small groups for youth and adults proliferate, and group-leader development is one of their highest priorities.

Adult/child theological studies, Promiseland Parks, puppets and black-light stars, children tutoring their peers and younger, children producing as well as consuming programming in their departments at church—what a tour! Each example includes a combination of high-energy relationship building and creativity sponsored by volunteers who understand how to apply small-group designs into an existing class.

Each example includes a combination of high-energy relationship building and creativity sponsored by volunteers who understand how to apply small-group designs into an existing class.

Where do we get our ideas about how to organize our members?

Before we get too excited about creative ways to energize and organize our congregations, let me address a couple of basic questions:

• How did we get to where we are now?

• Where do our most fundamental organizational ideas and models come from?

The Jewish Heritage

God's people have been gathering in both big and small meetings for a long time. Actually, Christians were gathering even before they were called Christians.

Christianity was never a "Lone Ranger" religion. Its roots were in the life of the tribes of Israel. When the Israelites came out of Egypt, they routinely worshipped in both large and small settings. Small meetings were with neighbors and by households in their respective villages. Their poet-king, David, called their really big meetings "the great congregation." Those huge gatherings, or feasts, were held several times a year next to their tabernacle and later at their temple in Jerusalem. During these feasts, they would celebrate their faith, receive instruction, and participate in various rites.

Defeated and dispersed by ancient warlords, the Jews had to learn to keep their faith alive wherever they were. Wherever ten Jewish households could be found, they organized a synagogue and called weekly meetings. A simple liturgy for the meetings included songs, reading the sacred writings we know as the Old Testament, exhortations, and observance of rites of passage. These dispersed worshippers of Jehovah planned and made pilgrimages to Jerusalem. In the centuries prior to Jesus, they saw their hopes for God's deliverance renewed by a restored temple, which they were using even as Jesus was born.

Jesus was Jewish. His people were going through hard times when he arrived. At the time of his birth, Jesus' family had to leave Palestine for a time to avoid persecution. When they brought Jesus back, he not only joined with his family to celebrate the big events, such as the feasts of Israel in Jerusalem, but in the smaller meetings at the synagogue in Nazareth as well.

The Christian Era

As the Christian faith spread, local Christian churches were organized much like synagogues. Indeed, many of the earliest Christian churches were splits out of Jewish synagogues. During the first centuries of the Christian era, only occasional large meetings were conducted, since Roman authorities often persecuted the new faith. As a result, Christians met in private homes, in what we now call "house churches." Their meetings often had to be conducted secretly, much as Chinese Christians have to do today. Leaders of those early house churches were volunteers because no clergy had been officially designated.

Where the government supported the Christian churches, huge worship centers were built, and elaborate public meetings with much pomp and ceremony became common. The times that followed are lost to us in the shadowy accounts we have from the Middle Ages. Not many leaps in technology or in the feudalism that governed everyday life occurred during those centuries, before the ages of global discovery.

When we come to the events that led up to our current understanding of the Christian movement, we look to our predecessors in the British Isles. As technology overshadowed feudalism and changed the face of the working world, many people were forced to move away from their birthplaces. They lost touch with their villages or parish churches and often lived in situations of great need. In response to their needs, new leaders arose within the Christian movement. These leaders were concerned that large numbers of common people were out of touch with the churches as well as the Gospel that was the core of the faith. Such leaders as George Whitfield and John Wesley took whatever opportunities they could to preach beyond their parish churches, even out-of-doors if necessary. Many, if not most, of those who responded had no current parish church connection.

To conserve the commitment of those who followed his teaching, Wesley instructed the new Christians to participate in weekly class meetings. Although Wesley was an ordained clergyman, lay workers, not clergy, led the class meetings he organized. In these meetings, time was allotted for participants to share their experiences and challenges. Those who were faithful in attending the small class meetings were invited to take part in the rites of larger services of divine worship held in parish churches and led by clergy.

The Sunday school developed as a training organization with a secret.

American Christianity developed into two primary types. Some Christian colonists brought their churches with them and focused at once on conducting worship and training their children in the faith. Other colonists and their children became Christian believers later under the influence of evangelists and revival movements. These new Christians, including many children, needed instruction in faith issues. Both types of churches adopted Sunday schools as their preferred way of training.

Over time, churches adopted educational methodologies that worked well in closely graded schools. Elaborate Christian education facilities were constructed. Lessons were written and published so that lay workers could assist in the training. The goal was to establish a class for every age and interest. These "little church meetings" appeared during the Sunday school hour, followed by the big meetings in a main auditorium where the senior minister preached.

Sunday school programs became the religious equivalent of the public school. They had superintendents, departments, teachers, classrooms, curricula, and attendance records. Leaders collected statistics for quality control, and they developed follow-up procedures to show concern for those who came and those who missed.

This emerging Sunday school was an industrial society invention. Conformity and uniformity assured that everyone would receive similar, consistent instruction. It assumed that the pupils were able and willing to grasp what was offered, and for many, the assumptions worked. Generations of biblically literate Christians owe their knowledge to Sunday school teachers.

The success of these Sunday school programs was not really in the teaching itself. Success had more to do with the settings that were created, where attitude toward learning was transformed. In the context of the small group, a teacher could show personal interest in each pupil. Questions could go both ways. Participants could show empathy, affection, and concern. Prayerful pastoral care could be rendered. If you attended one of those classes, the teachers would take time to listen to you because they cared. If you were absent, you were missed because they cared. These early classes demonstrated the truth that "people don't care how much you know until they know how much you care."

The success of these Sunday school programs was not really in the teaching itself. Success had more to do with the settings that were created where attitude toward learning was transformed.

Sunday school pupils who march from class to big church go ready to hear the Word of God taught and to celebrate God's presence. They've had many of their personal needs met, so they are open to the teaching of the pulpit. They are also connected socially so that whatever problems they might have with the pulpit teaching, they can work out in the interactive setting of the smaller class meeting where they have time to struggle with their questions.

Small Sunday school classes are really small groups.

All this is to say that a well-run Sunday school program is itself a small-group system but with some differences from home groups. If you keep the emphasis on small versus large, the small-group character of the Sunday school is easier to keep in view.

Small groups allow for lay workers to take part in leading them. Small groups provide a place for personal encouragement and for asking questions. Small groups assure that people aren't overlooked. Small groups allow for trust to build and for intimate thoughts and feelings to be shared. Small groups allow for contact time between leaders and participants. And small groups support large groups.

Large groups provide excitement and a sense of significance to those who participate in them. Participants and leaders of large groups benefit by knowing that there is a time and place for personal needs to be addressed, beyond the big meeting. Large groups are a place where platform performances can be impressive and enjoyable, even if contact with those who lead them is limited.

Sunday school is becoming a small-group network.

Today's Sunday school movement is evolving into something more like a small-group network. At a meeting called by Leadership Network, children's ministry leaders concluded, "Children's ministry in the future will include a greater emphasis on building relationships with children...Increasingly Sunday morning is viewed less as a "school" format and more as a time of shepherding and caregiving to children...more time in small groups for the purpose of nurture and relationship building." [1]

Early memories of church include Sunday school and small groups.

My earliest memories of church include Sunday school classes. I sang "I'll be a Sunbeam for Jesus" with the casual inattention of a three-year-old. Later I sharpened my Bible familiarization with aggressive competition in "sword drills" in which we earned recognition for the speed that we looked up and shouted out the first line of selected Bible verses.

By the time I was twelve, our class had earned a reputation as a teacher killer. In time there was a parade of timid volunteers retired from service, exhausted, after failing to keep order while shut in with a roomful of us during the Sunday school hour. My parents assured me that I *would* attend, in spite of my terrorist status. Not until the fateful day of my own Christian conversion did I cooperate. I can still remember the event because I found peace after praying at the altar. After weeks of excruciating conviction and fearfulness, I was led to a radical change in my behavior. In one weekend I moved from a management problem to an enthusiastic leader.

My early memories remind me that I did appreciate Sunday school. My heroes in the church were pastors and Christian educators who lauded the virtues of Sunday school.

When I became an adult, I attended Sunday school conventions, read Sunday school administration books, wrote Sunday school lessons, and organized a Sunday school in the new church development that my wife, Grace, and I led. I reveled in the stories of Sunday school history as it developed in England in mill villages as free literacy schools for impoverished children. My mentors praised the accomplishments of Sunday school pioneers, including the independent Baptist, Louis Entzminger, and the Southern Baptist, Arthur Flake. My father's personal readings were restricted largely to his Bible, his Hardware Age magazine, and his Baptist Sunday school lesson quarterly. From these he prepared lessons to teach the boys' classes he led for as many years as I can remember. Everything Elmer Towns wrote about the Sunday school was in my library and dog-eared from frequent reference.

My exposure to small groups was positive.

Before entering church-growth consulting in the late seventies, I was introduced to small groups through Lyman Coleman's earliest published resources. Faith at Work magazine was a prime source of inspiration. Ray Ortlund organized his prayer meetings around small breakout groups at the Lake Avenue Congregational Church in Pasadena, where visitors like me were exposed to prayer experiences that helped us to apply his preaching. And Cecil Osborne's psychological writings espoused the curative power of groups as microcommunities. He once said, "It takes people to make you sick and it takes people to help you get well." It was a creative time. We blissfully added small groups to our church program with excellent benefits and without toxic side effects.

Conflicts arose between Sunday school and small groups.

When I became a full-time consultant to churches, in the late seventies, I began witnessing the rise of tensions between Sunday school and small-group participants in churches.

At first the war between the stakeholders of the Sunday school (the establishment "old guard") and the innovators (the new barbarians of the small-group avant-garde) was heard as a distant din. As long as small groups were viewed in the same light as cottage prayer meetings and elective courses, they weren't a threat.

A notable experiment in transitioning an existing church in Albuquerque, New Mexico, led to a disastrous failure. The story was reported by denominational researchers in a widely circulated book about house churches and home cell groups. The backlash from threatened Sunday school stakeholders in that church led to a showdown that caused the staff to dismantle the cell group initiative permanently.

Author and pastor Ralph W. Neighbour Jr., who had studied small groups in the Asian context, forcefully championed the proposition that the future of the church would be found in small groups—not just any small group, but a particular type of small group that had been dubbed "cell groups" by Korean Pastor David Yonggi Cho, legendary founder of the largest local congregation in Christian history. Ralph knew a great deal about replicating good ministry. He used the methods he had learned from a denomination very successful in raising up lay leaders. He applied them and formulated a new plan for organizing a congregation. In contrast to a Sunday school-based church model, he called it the "pure cell church" model and offered to publish what he knew under a denominational board.

A funny thing happened on the way to headquarters, however, that left Ralph feeling betrayed. His offer to publish was canceled after he had made an irreversible commitment to the project. He suffered a severe financial setback because he had counted on the sponsorship of the publishers. Stung by the rejection of what Ralph saw as the only viable future for congregations, he wrote an influential and widely read book, *Where Do We Go From Here.* The tone of the book reflects some of the hurt he felt. It led to a polarization between traditional church leaders with their worship services and Sunday schools and the future-oriented church leaders who were willing to "pay the price" to develop "pure cell churches." These early cell churches were started from scratch, even in the face of considerable opposition. For Ralph, facing resistance and suffering casualties for what he believed to hold the future of the church was all part of the sacrifice that he, as a cell-group pioneer, had to make to be obedient to his calling.

For Ralph, facing resistance and suffering casualties for what he believed to hold the future of the church was all part of the sacrifice that he, as a cell-group pioneer, had to make to be obedient to his calling.

At one point, Uncle Ralph, as he's affectionately called by those who work closely with him, was invited to Singapore to help an outstanding young Chinese leader, Lawrence Khong, transform Faith Community Baptist Church into a cell-based church. The transformation worked very well, and FCBC grew to over six hundred groups in the nearly five years that Uncle Ralph worked with them.

Their successes reinforced his conviction that his cell-group model was the right one.

In recent years, Ralph has sponsored transitioning seminars in many cities across the nation. The tone of his presentations, however, is more hopeful about the ability of established churches to incorporate cells into traditional settings.

Is the clash really necessary?

While Ralph was in Singapore, Eddie Gibbs, professor of evangelism at Fuller Theological Seminary in Pasadena, wrote a book entitled *In Name Only: Tackling the Problem of Nominal Christianity.* Eddie's book is a road map for ministering in post-Christian society. He discovered that churches that organized Christians into cells could reach people living in a cultural milieu characterized by secularism. He calls these cells "small witnessing communities of faith."

Without attacking Sunday schools or other traditional programs, he cited numerous examples of such groups effectively changing lives in England and elsewhere. His writing added support to the notion that a successful future for the church would require small groups. Eddie didn't talk much in his book about the small-group/Sunday school conflict, partly because his gentle style just doesn't provoke controversy. Another reason may be that the British church leaders he worked with typically didn't have as much investment in adult Sunday school classes and didn't react toward home groups as strongly as their American counterparts did.

Another church leader who studied Dr. Cho and adopted his methods in America was Dale Galloway. Though Dale now heads a significant leadership center at Asbury Seminary, as a pastor he led his members in Portland to learn about ministry from lay pastors who led home cells. New Hope Community Church in Portland climbed to over five thousand in attendance with more than five hundred groups. He led the earliest and largest example of the Korean methods in North America. He was the founding pastor of New Hope, so transitioning was more a matter of casting a clear vision than of fighting off an old guard who felt threatened by changes. In other words, Dale's task wasn't as much a political challenge as it was a vision challenge. Thus, his teachings aren't regarded by Sunday school proponents as antagonistic to their work.

Discovering the real basis for the tensions

Meanwhile, my own consulting began taking me into churches that were distressed by tensions arising between the Sunday school and small-group program leaders. I vividly recall a congregation in the Midwest that gave me my first glimpse into the real nature of the struggle that was unfolding.

During a several-day visit to the congregation, the pastor glowingly outlined his dream for me. He envisioned a church where lay leaders would organize home Bible study and support groups that functioned as small cells. His enthusiasm was contagious. The church board and the rest of the staff appeared to support his vision. But there existed some underlying tensions, uneasiness, and unrest within the congregation. After numerous interviews, a picture emerged that helped me interpret the nature of the problem. The Sunday school organization was severely stressed by a chronic shortage of teachers and aides. The volunteer personnel needed to sustain the level of child care required by a growing church family was inadequate for the Sunday school program. Some of the Sunday school staff suggested that the shortage had been caused by all the volunteer workers being siphoned off by the pastor who was overseeing new members. Traditionally, each crop of new members had been drafted into the Sunday school. With the pastor's excitement about small-group ministry, many of the new members were being deployed as small-group leaders, and the Sunday school program was starving for workers. My investigation confirmed their suspicions.

What do Sunday school and small groups both offer?

To continue a fruitful discussion of the tensions that exist between Sunday school and small groups, it's helpful to ask, "What do Sunday school and small group programs both offer to the churches?" and "Can a vision for both be developed in a way that allows for cooperation rather than competition?"

In providing an answer, I believe it's most helpful to see a small-groups system in a soft-shelled Sunday school. This image requires that we imagine what a Sunday school program would look like if its classes couldn't all meet in one place at one time. The organizational chart for such a program would undoubtedly look very much like a traditional Sunday school organization chart. Each class with its pupils and teachers would be shown, grouped to reflect age or interest. The plans for study, such as the curriculum, would look no different.

The logistics for obtaining space to meet, transporting class members to each location, and gathering and consolidating reports from teachers would be no different from those any Boy or Girl Scout area director must arrange. Little League sports regional coordinators face the same hurdles.

What makes traditional Sunday school programs different are conveniences, such as compact, centralized facilities where teachers and pupils can gather. Teachers in the Sunday school also have an advantage because their pupils are typically delivered to them by the parents. Attendance is part of a larger activity, that of a family coming together for a morning at church. This is seen as a convenience for parents, who otherwise might have to make special trips to support their children's involvement.

A Sunday school program and a small-group program may be almost indistinguishable on an organization chart. Venue as well as meeting date and time are the only major differences.

Unfortunately, battle lines are usually drawn between Sunday school and small-group programs around competition for the scarcest commodity— the volunteer leaders.

Unfortunately, battle lines are usually drawn between Sunday school and small-group programs around competition for the scarcest commodity—the volunteer leaders.

This challenge actually provides a substantial opportunity to convert the competition into something very useful—the formation of more leaders for all programs. The most effective way to do this is to enlist current leaders to help create a new wave of leaders. This is known as *the apprentice system.*

Sunday school is an industrial-age organization

The culture of the developed world is in transition. The industrial era of power and mass production is giving way to a postmodern era driven by the digital revolution. The industrial era was characterized by uniformity arising from mass production. It was characterized in part by the smokestack factory and the closely graded school system with classes, methods, and rules.

While new postmodern technology may support personal treatment of people through a series of databases, it doesn't meet the human need for touch. As a result, the need for intimate relationships achieved through small groups is increasing.

The emerging era of postmodernism is challenging many aspects of these institutions and is characterized by the microprocessor and the Internet. Today's knowledge allows for customization of both production and learning. While new postmodern technology may support personal treatment of people through a series of databases, it doesn't meet the human need for touch. As a result, the need for intimate relationships achieved through small groups is increasing.

The Sunday school is an institution with roots in the industrial era. Its focus in American churches has been to assure biblical instruction and to catechize children. Its consumption of published curricula has resulted in profit centers for many denominations. These publishing activities and their finances create special interest groups of stakeholders who often perceive suggestions to change as a threat to their prosperity or existence. This includes new advances in understanding the learning process including the importance of focusing on doing what's best for the learner rather than what's best for the teacher or denomination.

Success in any curriculum-based program, including Sunday schools and small groups, requires a focus on the pupils and not just the lessons and program. Effective teachers create personal relationships rather than regimented and socially sterile environments, like those of traditional school classes. But remnants of factory and school cultures dictate that pupils be monitored for attendance, and like truant children, must be followed up on after a prescribed number of absences.

> *Success in any curriculum-based program, including Sunday schools and small groups, requires a focus on the pupils and not just the lessons and program.*

Related needs are met by both small groups and Sunday schools.

There are two primary needs that lead congregations to organize themselves into smaller social units. The first is the need of congregational members to be cared for and listened to. Opportunities to ask questions and to lodge concerns and to be known to others are invaluable in the formation of community. Members who can share what they think and feel and have their needs and opinions taken seriously by others develop a sense of belonging that contributes to their sense of well-being.

The second need is related to a feeling of personal significance gained by contributing to the care and well-being of others. There is a sense of effective stewardship that comes with accepting responsibility for leading others. Besides, every Christian has a need to serve in one capacity or another.

Both Sunday schools and small-group programs have a place in the postmodern church.

What both Sunday school and small-group programs in a particular congregation can do is to assure opportunities for intimate sharing

Small classes and groups can be of tremendous value in preparing future waves of leaders needed in all aspects of church life.

and leadership development. Small classes and groups can be of tremendous value in preparing future waves of leaders needed in all aspects of church life. Apprentice roles in both Sunday school and small-group programs can serve as very effective leadership incubators.

Near Kansas City there is a congregation that meets in a rented public school building. The pastor, David Pendleton, started Christ Community Church of the Nazarene as a mission church while he was serving as a staff member of a nearby existing church. Together with his wife and three children, another family of five, and a bunch of singles, the core group worshiped together for three months before entering the public realm. From a first public worship of 78, attendance climbed to a weekly average of 240. For the congregation's sixth anniversary celebration, there were more than 300 in attendance in a tent meeting that was nearly rained out.

Today, with a ten-acre campus purchased and paid for, the congregation will break ground for its first phase of facilities in mid-1999. Each Sunday morning the entire congregation, including children, meets together for opening songs and prayers. The children up through elementary grades are dismissed to conduct their own worship and drama miniservice, followed by breakout groups for discussion and prayers led by children's lay pastors.

David's concepts of moving teachers toward lay pastoring have been developed in dialogue with one of his mentors, Dale Galloway. While at Wilmore, Kentucky, David studied under Dale as an intern and, in the process, developed a vision for leadership development. David's concept of children's lay pastors is equivalent to children's Sunday school teachers, except that they're expected to develop relationships with their pupils by meeting with them during the week for recreation and other activities.

To date, four such microcommunities of faith have been formed. Christ Community Church in Olathe is another example. It provides a strong emphasis on leadership development, care groups, and blended worship. The enthusiastic staff and members have had a vision for the congregation as a worshipping community of faith from the beginning.

What differences exist between the Christ Community Church ministry model and a more traditional one? Organizational charts wouldn't necessarily reveal the differences because both list teachers and classes. The differences are related more to tone. Relationships are the key to the Christ Community Church organizational model. Staff spends much time developing relationships and conducting training meetings with lay pastors. Lay pastors make relationship building a high priority during group meetings and between meetings. The congregation worships together and then breaks into smaller groups for personal support. Material delivered in the sermon is carried into group life for further study and application to everyday life. Personal ministry to one another is evident.

Ironically, the lack of a Christian education classroom system has helped the congregation maintain its feeling of journeying together on a relational and spiritual pilgrimage as a people of God. Their life-changing experiences and their individual stories are the stuff of which their sense of community is built.

Such a case as Christ Community Church illustrates the essential similarity of Sunday school and small-group ministry. Effective relationships lead to a sense of belonging, which then leads participants to embrace the Gospel. Exposure to Christian education is important in a congregation, but unless intimate relationships are developed in the process, life-changing experiences will be lacking.

What is clear is that both Sunday school classes and small groups can be microcommunities. Both can offer support for their constituents. Both require leaders who are willing to act as pastors toward their groups. The differences between classes and groups can be stated very easily: Classes are typically held on-site with strict start and end times, whereas groups are generally held off-premises and hold meetings that are longer, with more casual beginning and end times.

Exposure to Christian education is important in a congregation, but unless intimate relationships are developed in the process, life-changing experiences will be lacking.

The "Zero Sum" Game

The only way some congregations get a new leader is when one transfers in from another city or church. As a result, these congregations often get caught up in a classic problem that I refer to as the "zero sum" game. This occurs when various programs are all bidding for the available talent, which, of course, is a finite sum. Here's how a zero sum game works. The equation is a simple one:

Supply of qualified leaders minus Sunday school teachers minus small-group leaders equals zero.

Let's assume the number of available leaders is fixed. When the number of leaders assigned to the Sunday school is known, let's say the remaining leaders are available for the small-group program. If ten leaders are available and six are in the Sunday school program, only four remain for the small-group program. If a fifth small-group leader is recruited from the pool, the Sunday school will have to make do with only five teachers. One program gets a leader at the expense of another program. That's the basis for war, as history has already demonstrated.

Waiting for new talent to join the church isn't an adequate strategy for churches that are serious about pursuing growth.

The resolution of this kind of dilemma is to pursue a strategy of growing more volunteer leaders for all programs. Waiting for new talent to join the church isn't an adequate strategy for churches that are serious about pursuing growth. New leaders must be cultivated from within the ranks of the current membership.

When Jim Dethmer, who served for several years as a teaching pastor at the Willow Creek Community Church near Chicago, worked with me in presenting seminars, he conducted one called "Advanced Small Groups." In that seminar he noted that the task of recruiting new leaders is often the responsibility of only a few people in a congregation, for example, the pastoral staff, the Sunday school superintendent, or perhaps the chairperson or members of a nominating committee. Jim notes that the number of leaders needed in a given congregation are so great that these few are simply not enough to handle recruiting needs.

I couldn't agree with Jim more. From the vantage point of seeing leadership shortages in churches of all types, the only sensible way to assure an adequate supply of new leaders is to develop them from within. In most congregations, the work force for recruiting and cultivating new leaders is already in place, but largely unrecognized. The best people in a congregation to recruit and train new leadership talent are the current active leaders. By mobilizing current leaders to help with this task, the potential to create new leaders is enormous.

Develop a strategy to enlarge the leadership team.

The challenge, then, is to develop a strategy to bring current leaders on board. How to accomplish this has been the focus of my study for the past five years. After several years of experimentation, it's clear that some very simple methods, if consistently used, will break the drought of the leader supply in a congregation.

The first step is to gently renegotiate the role of your current leaders to include bringing an apprentice leader alongside as they serve. A new role, that of leader-in-training, needs to be inserted into the language of volunteer workers in congregations. Envision, for a moment, a church in which every team, group, committee, board, and class leader is preparing new leaders. In such a church, every leader would become a leader-maker. Current leaders would allow newly emerging talent to take over their jobs while they take a break or undertake a new leadership position, or new leadership talent could be transferred and assigned to other areas. This is the most certain way to break out of the zero sum game—to develop once again the number of leaders that you already have.

In virtually every congregation I have studied, most of the ministry is done by 10 percent of the active participants. These diligent souls work with two, three, or four hats each, sacrificing a lot and complaining little. In every congregation that I have studied, I've also detected the presence of another group as large as or larger than the active group. This second group is an invisible army of willing but reluctant workers. They stand back and watch for a suitable invitation to help with something that they feel is within their range of ability. They take one look at the overworked 10 percent and they're not sure they want to take part in a position of leadership. Many of these invisible ones are very capable, but they lack a reasonable pathway into a position of leadership that will assure their success.

Once solidly enrolled and trained, this second group will serve with distinction and faithfulness, and if appropriately challenged, they will make the zero sum game unnecessary. These future leaders require good examples of effective leadership and positive relational support while they are learning to lead. If trained through an apprentice program, this group will quickly become the backbone of tomorrow's volunteer work force.

The reinterpretation of the role of your leaders to include apprenticing is a vital first step; it begins by casting a vision. As with anything new, however, it has the potential to produce a firestorm of resistance at first. My recommendation is to introduce the concept in a way that will minimize the anxiety and the resistance of the current leadership. This can best be done by including two components in early development stages:

1. Avoid making premature announcements; and
2. Coach leaders individually until apprentices are in place.

In most cases, leaders can identify potential apprentices within their existing groups.

In most cases, leaders can identify potential apprentices within their existing groups. If not, they can be assisted in finding suitable apprentice talent from elsewhere in the congregation.

Use coaching tools to recruit and train apprentices.

Working with pastoral staff in churches of all sizes has led me to observe a very wide range of skill in coaching current leaders about recruiting and training apprentices. For many leaders, coaching is not innate.

In response to this apparent deficiency, I typically direct the congregations I work with to one of two tools that have proven to be effective. The first tool is a series of nine commitments. It's been published in two formats: a video library and a book. The commitments expand the role of group leaders by formally renegotiating what is expected of them. The other tool, an interview structure for coaching, also deals with many of these same issues, including finding and nurturing an apprentice to maturity.

These nine commitments are found in my book, *Nine Keys to Effective Small Group Leadership,* which is based on my video series: *Nine Facets of the Effective Small Group Leader:*

• I will be available for debriefing interviews with the church staff.

• I will recruit my replacement(s) before we begin meeting with the group, and I will help my replacement(s) develop an ability to lead.

• I will reach out between meetings, cultivating both old and new contacts.

• I will prepare my mind and heart for our meetings and will include my apprentice(s) in the process.

• I will conduct meetings that encourage believers and accept seekers.

• I will bring group members to worship for the church's weekend services.

• I will serve others with my gifts, knowledge, energy, time, and money, conscious that my greatest influence may occur as I set an example.

• I will make time to build acquaintances with unbelievers, serving them at their points of struggle.

• I will meet regularly with God in private prayer.

The tutoring process for the commitments is guided by a series of video recordings designed to be viewed with a pastoral staff member or other coach. Each session is broken into

The wave of the future is in developing congregations into unified bodies where relationships are a high priority in all small groups. This includes promoting closeness, warmth, and support in all groups, including Sunday school classes.

equal parts of viewing and discussing the material.

The other tool, a structured interview comprised of twenty-eight questions guides the coaching process. It is used to establish a quality encounter between group leaders and their coaches that results in affirmation and mutual problem solving.

Information about these tools is available by e-mail request from carlgeorge@metachurch.com or by calling 1-800-936-2368.

Ten Steps for Organizing and Developing Small-Group Leadership

1. Develop a wall chart with a circle for each class or group under your supervision. Make each circle of a size that is proportional to the group's average attendance when it meets. Label it with its class name and teacher/leader name.

2. Mark each circle with a symbol to indicate the presence of apprentice leaders. Use a separate "Xa" to indicate each apprentice leader in a group. This symbol combines the Roman numeral for 10, which is the average size of classes and groups combined with the first letter of the word apprentice. If some groups have several apprentices, use several indicators.

3. Place a sticky tab on each group with the most recent date its teacher or leader was interviewed by a supervisor or coach. By changing colors of the sticky tab each month, you can see at a glance how long ago the most recent interviews were conducted.

4. Summarize and report regularly to church staff and boards progress in interviewing leaders and placing apprentices. (A format that clearly shows how to visualize trends in these two measures can be downloaded free from my Web site at www.metachurch.com. See the "Tracking Progress of Coaching of Group Leaders.")

5. Use a structured interview format to develop a helping relationship with each leader. You may request a free reproducible sample questionnaire by e-mail from carlgeorge@metachurch.com. You may also request the information by fax from (909) 396-6845, or instantly

download a copy by calling that number from the phone attached to a fax machine.

6. Use the 3-2-1 training method (three seats, two interviews, and one reflection time) to train and support coaches. In this method, one seat is for a coach to model an interview with a group leader, who is seat two. The third seat is for a coach-in-training, who conducts a second interview with a second group leader while being observed by the modeling coach. Reflections on these interviews are then shared by the coach and coach-in-training.

7. Help leaders reinterpret their roles to include expecting to be coached, to develop apprentice leaders, and to strengthen relationships within their groups. Meeting and keeping in touch between meetings best accomplish this.

An excellent tool to help with this is my book *Nine Keys to Effective Small Group Leadership.* In addition, a new method called tutored video instruction (TVI) has been developed in a video series called *Nine Facets of Effective Small Group Leaders.* It's used in small clusters of two to five leaders-in-training to progress through the concepts in five-minute segments. (Information on this nine-video series is available by calling 1-800-936-2368 or from the author's Web site: www.metachurch.com.)

8. Utilize spiritual gifts identification tools to help prospective class teachers and group leaders discover their special abilities. (A selection of these tools can be obtained by calling the ICLDE in British Columbia at 1-800-804-0777, publishers of the original *Houts Spiritual Gifts Questionnaire* and the Wesley version of the same.)

9. Set up a liaison with new member classes so new prospective leaders are oriented to your apprentice program as an entry point for their volunteer service.

10. Arrange times for coaches and teachers or leaders to meet for mutual support and ongoing training. Rather than a traditional staff lecture during this time, provide time for leaders to share their journeys, including both their joys and difficulties.

Nurture leaders for the future through coaching.

Sunday school advocates typically approach their task in *organization* terms. Sunday schools typically begin with a gathered people who are at church for a worship service. The apparent need is to organize worshipers into small groups to involve them in learning and discussion.

Small-group advocates, on the other hand, typically approach their tasks in family terms and focus on *building relationships.* They add lessons to give it a sense of progress and urge attendance in a larger worship setting to give participants a larger sense of significance.

The wave of the future is in developing congregations into unified bodies where relationships are a high priority in all groups. This includes promoting closeness, warmth, and support in all groups, including Sunday school classes. The key is to challenge existing leaders to bring coaching relationships into their groups. New leaders can be effectively nurtured and trained for positions of leadership through an apprentice program.

Endnotes

1. From NetFax #111. Quoted by permission of Leadership Network.

Group Publishing, Inc.
Attention: Product Development
P.O. Box 481
Loveland, CO 80539
Fax: (970) 679-4370

Evaluation for
New Directions for Small-Group Ministry

Please help Group Publishing, Inc., continue to provide innovative and useful resources for ministry. Please take a moment to fill out this evaluation and mail or fax it to us. Thanks!

● ● ●

1. As a whole, this book has been (circle one)

not very helpful   very helpful

| 1 | 2 | 3 | 4 | 5 | 6 | 7 | 8 | 9 | 10 |

2. The best things about this book:

3. Ways this book could be improved:

4. Things I will change because of this book:

5. Other books I'd like to see Group publish in the future:

6. Would you be interested in field-testing future Group products and giving us your feedback? If so, please fill in the information below:

Name _____

Street Address _____

City _____ State _____ Zip _____

Phone Number _____ Date _____

Exciting Resources for Your Adult Ministry

Sermon-Booster Dramas

Tim Kurth

   Now you can deliver powerful messages in fresh, new ways. Set up your message with memorable, easy-to-produce dramas—each just 3 minutes or less! These 25 low-prep dramas hit hot topics ranging from burnout...ethics...parenting...stress...to work...career issues and more! Your listeners will be on the edge of their seats!

ISBN 0-7644-2016-X

Fun Friend-Making Activities for Adult Groups
Karen Dockrey

More than 50 relational programming ideas help even shy adults talk with others at church! You'll find low-risk Icebreakers to get adults introduced and talking...Camaraderie-Builders that help adults connect and start talking about what's really happening in their lives...and Friend-Makers to cement friendships with authentic sharing and accountability.

ISBN 0-7644-2011-9

Bore No More (For Every Pastor, Speaker, Teacher)
Mike & Amy Nappa

   This is a must-have for pastors, college/career speakers, and others who address groups! Because rather than just provide illustrations to entertain audiences, the authors show readers how to involve audiences in the learning process. The 70 sermon ideas presented are based on New Testament passages, but the principles apply to all passages.

ISBN 1-55945-266-8

Young Adult Faith-Launchers

   These 18 in-depth Bible studies are perfect for young adults who want to strengthen their faith and deepen their relationships. They will explore real-world issues...ask the tough questions...and along the way turn casual relationships into supportive, caring friendships. Quick prep and high involvement make these the ideal studies for peer-led Bible studies, small groups, and classes.

ISBN 0-7644-2037-2

Bible Study Series

Give Your Teenagers a Solid Faith Foundation That Lasts a Lifetime!

Here are the *essentials* of the Christian life—core values teenagers *must* believe to make good decisions now...and build an *unshakable* lifelong faith. Developed by youth workers like you...field-tested with *real* youth groups in *real* churches...here's the meat your kids *must* have to grow spiritually—presented in a fun, involving way!

Each 4-session **Core Belief Bible Study Series** book lets you easily...
● Lead deep, compelling, *relevant* discussions your kids won't want to miss...
● Involve teenagers in exploring life-changing truths...
● Help kids create healthy relationships with each other—and you!

Plus you'll make an *eternal difference* in the lives of your kids as you give them a solid faith foundation that stands firm on God's Word.

Here are the Core Belief Bible Study Series titles already available...

Senior High Studies

Why **Authority** Matters	0-7644-0892-5
Why **Being a Christian** Matters	0-7644-0883-6
Why **Creation** Matters	0-7644-0880-1
Why **Forgiveness** Matters	0-7644-0887-9
Why **God** Matters	0-7644-0874-7
Why **God's Justice** Matters	0-7644-0886-0
Why **Jesus Christ** Matters	0-7644-0875-5
Why **Love** Matters	0-7644-0889-5
Why **Our Families** Matter	0-7644-0894-1
Why **Personal Character** Matters	0-7644-0885-2
Why **Prayer** Matters	0-7644-0893-3
Why **Relationships** Matter	0-7644-0896-8
Why **Serving Others** Matters	0-7644-0895-X
Why **Spiritual Growth** Matters	0-7644-0884-4
Why **Suffering** Matters	0-7644-0879-8
Why **the Bible** Matters	0-7644-0882-8
Why **the Church** Matters	0-7644-0890-9
Why **the Holy Spirit** Matters	0-7644-0876-3
Why **the Last Days** Matter	0-7644-0888-7
Why **the Spiritual Realm** Matters	0-7644-0881-X
Why **Worship** Matters	0-7644-0891-7

Junior High/Middle School Studies

The Truth About **Authority**	0-7644-0868-2
The Truth About **Being a Christian**	0-7644-0859-3
The Truth About **Creation**	0-7644-0856-9
The Truth About **Developing Character**	0-7644-0861-5
The Truth About **God**	0-7644-0850-X
The Truth About **God's Justice**	0-7644-0862-3
The Truth About **Jesus Christ**	0-7644-0851-8
The Truth About **Love**	0-7644-0865-8
The Truth About **Our Families**	0-7644-0870-4
The Truth About **Prayer**	0-7644-0869-0
The Truth About **Relationships**	0-7644-0872-0
The Truth About **Serving Others**	0-7644-0871-2
The Truth About **Sin and Forgiveness**	0-7644-0863-1
The Truth About **Spiritual Growth**	0-7644-0860-7
The Truth About **Suffering**	0-7644-0855-0
The Truth About **the Bible**	0-7644-0858-5
The Truth About **the Church**	0-7644-0899-2
The Truth About **the Holy Spirit**	0-7644-0852-6
The Truth About **the Last Days**	0-7644-0864-X
The Truth About **the Spiritual Realm**	0-7644-0857-7
The Truth About **Worship**	0-7644-0867-4

Order today from your local Christian bookstore, or write:
Group Publishing, P.O. Box 485, Loveland, CO 80539.

BRING THE BIBLE TO LIFE FOR YOUR 1ST- THROUGH 6TH-GRADERS...
WITH GROUP'S HANDS-ON BIBLE CURRICULUM™
Energize your kids with Active Learning!

Group's **Hands-On Bible Curriculum**™ will help you teach the Bible in a radical new way. It's based on Active Learning—the same teaching method Jesus used.

In each lesson, students will participate in exciting and memorable learning experiences using fascinating gadgets and gizmos you've not seen with any other curriculum. Your elementary students will discover biblical truths and <u>remember</u> what they learn because they're <u>doing</u> instead of just listening.

You'll save time and money, too!

While students are learning more, you'll be working less—simply follow the quick and easy instructions in the **Teacher Guide**. You'll get tons of material for an energy-packed 35- to 60-minute lesson. And, if you have extra time, there's an arsenal of Bonus Ideas and Time Stuffers to keep kids occupied—and learning! Plus, you'll SAVE BIG over other curriculum programs that require you to buy expensive separate student books—all student handouts in Group's **Hands-On Bible Curriculum** are photocopiable!

In addition to the easy-to-use **Teacher Guide**, you'll get all the essential teaching materials you need in a ready-to-use **Learning Lab**®. No more running from store to store hunting for lesson materials—all the active-learning tools you need to teach 13 exciting Bible lessons to any size class are provided for you in the **Learning Lab**.

Challenging topics each quarter keep your kids coming back!

Group's **Hands-On Bible Curriculum** covers topics that matter to your kids and teaches them the Bible with integrity. Switching topics every month keeps your 1st-through 6th-graders enthused and coming back for more. The full two-year program will help your kids...

- •make God-pleasing decisions,
- •recognize their God-given potential, and
- •seek to grow as Christians.

Take the boredom out of Sunday school, children's church, and midweek meetings for your elementary students. Make your job easier and more rewarding with no-fail lessons that are ready in a flash. Order Group's **Hands-On Bible Curriculum** for your 1st- through 6th-graders today.

Hands-On Bible Curriculum is also available for
Toddlers & 2s, Preschool, and Pre-K and K!

Order today from your local Christian bookstore, or write: Group Publishing, P.O. Box 485, Loveland, CO